ANTONÍN DVOŘÁK

ANTONÍN DVOŘÁK

LETTERS
AND REMINISCENCES

OTAKAR ŠOUREK

Translated from the Czech by
Roberta Finlayson Samsour

Artia · Prague

FOREWORD

Antonín Dvořák needs no introduction to the English-speaking public, for, during his life-time, no country honoured him more for his art nor paid greater tribute to his genius than England, while three years of his life were dedicated to work as a composer and teacher in America. Nor has his reputation suffered any decline in the estimation of succeeding generations, for Dvořák's name has its secure place among those of the world's greatest classics.

The unique course of Antonín Dvořák's life story, from the lowliest of beginnings to the highest rungs of fame—a story which the reader of this volume is enabled to follow through the skilful selection and arrangement of the letters and reminiscences made by Otakar Šourek, the leading Czech authority on Dvořák's life and work—while itself of no small interest, is enhanced by the picture it gives of his relations with notable personalities of the musical world of his day. Among these his friendship with Brahms stands out as one of the most beautiful friendships to be recorded between two great artists. Other letters, again, show the bond of warm mutual esteem that united Dvořák and his great Russian contemporary, Tchaikovsky, or the high respect for his genius shown by Gustav Mahler, in the presentation of Dvořák's works to the Viennese public. Here he was following in the tradition of his predecessor, Hans Richter, conductor of the Vienna Philharmonic, guest conductor of Europe's famous orchestras, later, permanent conductor of the Hallé orchestra in Manchester and one of Dvořák's most enthusiastic admirers and interpreters, the correspondence with whom has added interest as frequently throwing light on Dvořák's own estimation of his works. Other conductors, whose personal friendship he enjoyed and who also did much to bring his works to the notice of the musical public, are Hans von Bülow, Arthur Nikisch of Leipzig, Joseph Barnby, founder and conductor of the oratorio concerts in the Albert Hall, and Anton Seidl of New York. Ties of affection and professional interest were close, too, between Dvořák and many of the great reproductive artists of the time, such as Josef Joachim, violin virtuoso and leader of his own Quartet, to whom he dedicated his Violin Concerto, Hanuš Wihan, the noted Czech 'cellist, František Ondříček, the Czech violin virtuoso, the famous English oratorio singers, the Bohemian Quartet, the Hellmesberger Quartet in Vienna, the Kneisel Quartet in Boston, all of whom were happy to include the works of Dvořák in their programmes to which audiences in all parts of the world reacted with the same warm enthusiasm and admiration.

The reminiscences, again, illuminate different aspects of Dvořák's musicianship, his abilities as a conductor and as a pianist, while his valuable pedagogical work is reflected with great charm in the reminiscences of his pupils, among whom Josef Suk and Vítězslav Novák hold high place in the succeeding generation of Czech composers. Nor are there lacking those which give us intimate glimpses of the artist's personal traits.

These, however, are revealed best of all in Dvořák's own letters, which are written with that simplicity, sincerity and spontaneity which give them their distinctive flavour and charm. We get a picture of him as a loving and beloved father in the circle of his large family, for whom he is deeply concerned to make proper provision, as we learn from his very characteristic letters to his Berlin publisher, Simrock; we see the great-heartedness of his love and almost child-like affection for his friends, whose sympathy and interest are as necessary for his spiritual well-being as the lovely pine-forests of his country for his physical; we follow him in his struggle to dedicate his gifts to the highest aims of art and his stubborn refusal to make any compromise or take one step along the easier path to material success; we see him happy and inspired to new effort by appreciation and recognition, and hurt, but not dismayed, by malicious criticism or lack of understanding; we see him, too, in his intense preoccupation with his art and learn something of his methods of work; or, again, as a conscientious and enthusiastic teacher, who spares his pupils as little as he spares himself; and we cannot but wonder at the amazing industry, the ceaseless creative activity, which was never merely on the surface, but had its roots deep in his immense spiritual and musical resources. And, finally, there emerges the portrait of Dvořák, "a simple Czech musician", unspoiled by fame, with the manly virtues of truthfulness, courage and simplicity, a boundless enthusiasm for the beautiful, in whom love of God, love of his fellow-men and love of country (to each and all of which he acknowledged his debt with the true humility of greatness), were the mainsprings of a life dedicated with an unusual singleness of purpose to the service of art as his form of service to humanity.

If this volume, in spite of the transposition into another language, in which process some of the subtler and more volatile essences must needs escape, brings the life and work of Antonín Dvořák nearer to the reader, increases his insight into the mind and endears to him the personality of a genius to whom the whole world, in its turn, owes a debt, then those who have worked at the making of this book will be rewarded in knowing it to serve the purpose which they had in mind.

The Translator

9

The book which we here present to the public does not aim at giving a critical appreciation and analysis of the greatness, nature and significance of the creative personality of Antonín Dvořák. Its purpose—a much simpler but an equally rewarding one—is to illustrate by means of *documents, excerpts from memoirs* and *letters* written by Dvořák's contemporaries or by himself how altogether unique was the *life* of this artistic genius in its imposing rise from the humblest of Czech origins to the towering significance of an artist admired and honoured by the whole world, a life whose course is all the more remarkable when we consider how unassuming in its simple humanity, yet at the same time how inexpressibly noble, straightforward and pure was the *character* of its hero.

This collection of documents, the contents and names of the authors of which are themselves sufficient evidence of what outstanding contemporaries Dvořák counted among his friends and how high these personalities valued his art, brings out the unique nature of the events and circumstances of Dvořák's life and delineates his personal traits with all the greater warmth, conviction and interest the farther the idea was from the writers' minds, that these reminiscences and letters would one day fulfil such a mission. The general picture that thus emerges acquires its special colouring from the way it places in the foreground the exceptional greatness of Dvořák's *life-work*, which stamps its author as one of the most fertile and original creative spirits which Czech music has ever had or is ever likely to have.

The wealth of documentary material which I have collected in the course of long years devoted to the study of Dvořák's life and the critical evaluation of his work is, however, so great that it would provide material for several such books as this. And I must confess that only the necessity of keeping within the limits laid down by a book of this kind reconciled me to excluding many a document not less characteristic and interesting. I trust, however, that even within this narrower selection it has been possible for me to present the material in such a way as to bring out with plasticity the chief events in Dvořák's life and indicate the continuity of his artistic development, while at the same time illuminating sufficiently clearly the most characteristic features of his creative personality.

O. Š.

Prague, 18 9/1 86.

Honoured Sir,

I must confess quite frankly that I was rather taken aback by your esteemed letter because of its excessive devoutness and humility, so that it would seem as if you were speaking to some demigod, for which, however, I have never taken myself nor never shall.

I am just an ordinary Czech musician, who does not love such exaggerated humbleness, and although I have moved quite enough in the great musical world, I still remain what I have always been— a simple Czech musician.

Antonín Dvořák

...Among living composers of music, I know no other name able to set all the strings of my inner being vibrating in the same way.

Antonín Dvořák!

I yield myself up completely and willingly to the intoxicating sound of his lyre. When listening to his works, I lose all power of criticism and become a mere listener with nerves tingling to their very tips in sympathy—singing, weeping, rejoicing and dreaming along with him, forgetting for a fleeting moment the burden of existence and its infinite sadness...

Josef Bohumil Foerster *(see 15)*.

Truth ungilded, true democracy, not humbling himself before the mighty, not stressing his own greatness as compared with "lower" beings, the self-confidence of "one of the chosen" without vanity, feeling without sentimentality, an inexpressible delight in work, a pure and uncomplicated relation to God and his fellow-creatures —these were the qualities of his spirit.

And a continual creative restlessness! I see the Master's hand constantly, and often even during conversation in the intervals, playing restlessly on his coat as on a keyboard. It seemed as if his whole thought was only music.

He lived in the confident assurance that he was serving his Nation and his God...

The expression of his eyes was that of a child and at the same time that of a great and deeply reserved thinker, and if those eyes rested on yours in the abstraction of thought, involuntarily your inner being trembled...

Josef Suk *(see 1).*

...You know the feeling when somebody takes the word out of your mouth before you have time to form it? That was always my experience in Dvořák's company. In him his person and his work were interchangeable. And then his melodies were as if he had taken them from my heart. Such a bond nothing on earth can sever...

Leoš Janáček *(see 14).*

14

1. SUK'S LEGEND OF DVOŘÁK'S BIRTH

Near the spot where the Vltava joins the Labe (Elbe), below a proud castle, a boy was born in a poor cottage. It is late in the evening, the father is still at work outside, the mother by the cradle is humming softly till the infant falls asleep and her own tired, anxious eyes close in weariness. The cottage is silent except for the monotonous ticking of the old clock.

Suddenly in the gloaming there appear three strange female figures around the cradle. The three Old Women.

The first bends over the babe, kisses him on the forehead and says: "Much suffering and hardship will be your lot, but you will be strong and great. You shall forget all your poverty and though poor you shall give others happiness and wealth. Your thought and your work will bring a smile to people's faces and tears of gladness to their eyes."

The second figure then approaches, kisses the babe on the mouth and says: "Your lips shall not speak a sweet, smooth language. Yet in one word of yours there will be more wisdom than in whole books by men wise in their own conceit. You will be silent in days of greatest trial and of greatest joy."

And the third figure, beautiful beyond imagination, kisses the babe on the heart and says: "You shall be raised to a place among the greatest of your country's sons by the power of your understanding and the strength of your feeling. Your work shall be eternal, but be warned that work which bears the mark of immortality cannot be grasped by passing vanity. Son of this soil, know that the outside world will pay you homage and in you will pay homage to your country, but it is in your own country that you will experience many a disappointment. But your spirit will not be warped by wrath or bitterness—for you shall remain a child with the same pure spirit as you have today."

The babe began crying and the mother kissed the frightened child and comforted it.—*This is the legend of Nelahozeves…*

From the burial oration at the Vyšehrad Cemetery in Prague. *Josef Suk* (1874-1935), a noted Czech composer and, for 40 years, second violin in the widely famed Bohemian Quartet, was Dvořák's pupil and son-in-law.—Dvořák's birthplace was the small village of *Nelahozeves*, situated on the bank of the Vltava about 30 km north of Prague. Dvořák's father, František, and his wife, Anna, rented an inn here with a butcher's business. Their son, Antonín, was born as the first of nine children on the 8th September 1841.

2. DVOŘÁK'S RECOLLECTIONS OF CHILDHOOD

"…Look there at the little village with the long name of Nelahozeves. And there just below the castle of the Prince Lobkowitz, that low building…do you see it?—that's where my father had his inn and at the same time carried on his trade of butcher. It was in that little house that I was born and here in this lovely countryside that I spent my poor childhood."

The Master's voice sounded strangely soft… he fell silent for a while and his dark moist eyes wandered over the familiar scene. Suddenly his gaze came to rest on a particular point and round his lips there played a roguish smile. "The little church there... that's where I played my first violin solo. And what a fuss I was in that time and how afraid I was when I tuned my fiddle and how my bow shook at the first notes. But it turned out all right. When I had finished, there was a hum and buzz throughout the whole choir, everybody pressed round me—my friends smiled happily at me and clapped me good-naturedly on the shoulder, and our neighbour, the leader of the violins, gave me a whole groschen."

"That was the happier side of my youth, the brighter moments, but even the darker side was not uninteresting though it cost me many a tear. Look there! These are the places I used to visit with my Father to buy all kinds of cattle-beasts, and when my Father entrusted me with one or other member of the brute creation, it would often out of sheer exuberence give me the slip, or without more ado drag me into the nearest pond, so that my situation was not exactly enviable. But all the calamities and trials of my young life were sweetened by music, my guardian angel... That little church on the hill there, is my old acquaintance. There, at fair times, I would play under the leadership of the brother of my Zlonice teacher, Liehmann, who was choirmaster here..."

From the book of reminiscences: "With Dvořák in England", by *Václav J. Novotný* (1849-1922), Czech composer, writer and critic. In September,1884, he accompanied Dvořák on his second visit to England to the musical festival in Worcester (see 85-86). For a note on the teacher, Antonín Liehmann, see 4.

3. CERTIFICATE OF APPRENTICESHIP ISSUED BY THE BUTCHER'S GUILD IN ZLONICE

We, the undersigned office-holders of the honourable Town Guild of Butchers,

do by these presents bear witness and confirm that Antonín Dvořák of Nelahozeves, born on the 8th September 1841, of Roman Catholic denomination, was bound as an apprentice in the year 1854, on the

fifth of the month of November, at the opening of the Guild Fund,
to the butcher's trade, the apprenticeship to run from the 1st November
for two years.—In as far as the aforesaid Antonius Dvořák conducted
himself during the specified period of the two years of his apprentice-
scip honestly, faithfully and industriously, and having learned, as is
testified to by his Master, Jan Roubal, the trade of butcher well and
properly, he was presented on the self-same 1st of November 1856
to the assembled gathering, under the chairmanship of the P. T.
superintendant of this Guild and declared in due order to have served
his apprenticeship.

Having made out for the above-named Antonius Dvořák this
CERTIFICATE OF APPRENTICESHIP entitling him to carry
on the trade of butcher, we beg that he should be recognized as a
properly taught butcher's journeyman and everywhere received with
courtesy. In witness whereof this certificate of apprenticeship is
awarded him by the undersigned and under the Guild Seal Ordinary.
On the 2nd November 1856.

Jan Roubal

Jan Warský, Frantz Ekert,
Josef Bjlej,
Certified Master,

Jan Bílý
Building Master and Teacher.

In the years 1854-1856, in the little town of Zlonice by Slaný in Bohemia, Dvořák
learned the trade of butcher and was, at the same time, a pupil of the organist Antonín
Liehmann (see 4). There he continued with his violin lessons and acquired his first
knowledge of piano and organ.—He then spent the school-year 1856-57 in Česká
Kamenice, where he improved his German and went on with his musical training.

4. DVOŘÁK'S TEACHER IN ZLONICE

The Zlonice choir-master, Antonín Liehmann, whose name
has been saved from oblivion through its link with the name of
Dvořák, must have been an interesting character if we are to

judge from the Master's description which is as follows: "Lieh-mann was a good musician, but he was quick-tempered and still taught according to the old methods: if a pupil could not play a passage, he got as many cuffs as there were notes on the sheet... He was well versed in harmony—though of course his notions of harmony were different from those of the present day—and he had a good grasp of thorough bass: he could also read and play figured bass fluently and taught us to do the same. But it often happened that where there were more figures, and among them several with strokes, before you could work it out you had received three boxes on the ear..."

From a book of recollections gleaned from Dvořák's own telling ("Z Dvořákova vyprávění") by *Josef Michl*, one of Dvořák's pupils at the school of composition in the Prague Conservatoire, who wrote a number of delightful recollections of Dvořák as a teacher. *Antonín Liehmann* (1808-1879), teacher, organist and choir-master in Zlonice, a good country musician and composer. It was chiefly thanks to his influence that Dvořák was able to give up the butcher's trade and devote himself to music as a profession (see also 3).

5. RECOLLECTIONS OF DVOŘÁK'S YOUTH

Toníček (Tony) had scarcely learned to walk when he was given the apron and hatchet that are the insignia of the butcher's trade. His grandmother loved the little boy and called him: "My little toothy", for Antonín, like almost all the members of the Dvořák family, had very good teeth. His grandmother died, however, in a few years. As a child, Antonín used to play to the guests—and when he was to give a "concert", what a bustle and to-do there was with the preparations. My cousin Františka helped my aunt in the business at that time and used to relate, even after the composer's death, what a timid child he was. Once before one of his concerts he broke a plate and was so upset about it that it was only with difficulty that he could be consoled. Here already his highly-strung nervous temperament was apparent. Uncle, however, in accordance with the family tradition, destined his sons for the butcher's trade; there were five of them, and then three sisters. But it was mainly due to the influence of his teacher, Liehmann, that Uncle was induced to release him from following the family calling and to give him to music. And so it was with respect and gratitude that the teacher Liehmann was remembered and often called to mind in our family. When Antonín showed little promise of taking to the butchery business, Uncle at last resolved to act and took the boy to Prague. (At that time Uncles used to walk to Prague even from Veltrusy.)

From that time, Antonín Dvořák was, with only short breaks, a member of our family till he got married—a period of about 15 years.

From a book of recollections ("Za Antonínem Dvořákem") by *Anna Dušková*, Dvořák's cousin. Dvořák lived with her parents in Prague up to his marriage in 1873. Dvořák's grandmother: *Anna Dvořáková* (1775-1848), a woman of refined disposition with an artistic taste in embroidery.

6. DVOŘÁK AT THE PRAGUE ORGAN-SCHOOL

Dvořák did not look back on the time he spent at the organ-school in Prague with any great pleasure; in fact the reference he makes to it has a bitter flavour.

"At the organ-school everything smelt of mould. Even the organ. Anybody who warted to learn anything had to know German. Anyone who knew German well could be dux of the class, but if he did not know German he could not be dux. My knowledge of German was poor, and even if I knew something I could not get it out. My fellow-pupils looked a little 'down their noses' at me and laughed at me behind their backs. And later on they still laughed at me. When they discovered that I was composing, they said among themselves: 'Just imagine that Dvořák! Do you know that he composes too?' And all those who laughed at me got on better than I did..."

From the book of recollections by *Josef Michl*, cited above (see 4).—Dvořák attended the organ-school in Prague, called "The Institute for Church Music" (founded 1830, in the years 1857-59 under the directors Karel F. Pietsch and Josef Krejčí). The German régime at the Institute was maintained by Krejčí, whose classification of Dvořák is given under no. 7.

7. EXTRACT FROM DVOŘÁK'S REPORT

An excellent but more practical talent. Practical knowledge and accomplishment seem to be his aim. In theory somewhat weaker...

8. DVOŘÁK'S STUDIES AT THE ORGAN-SCHOOL

... Of his studies at the Organ-school Dvořák rarely spoke in after years. It would seem that the school served him more as a means towards acquiring the formal training for the title of musician than the road to his vocation as a composer. Dvořák never underrated the solid theoretical grounding the Organ-school gave him, but the highest kind of musical learning he acquired outside of school.

From "Recollections of Antonín Dvořák" by *Dr Josef Zubatý*. Zubatý, later Professor in the Charles University of Prague, an outstanding Czech linguist (1855-1931), was an excellent musician and a great admirer of Dvořák, in the first years of whose rise to world fame he carried out the piano arrangements of orchestral and chamber works without his name being mentioned in the published editions. He also wrote Dvořák's first biography (published in German, Leipzig 1881).

9. DVOŘÁK JOINS AN ORCHESTRA

It is 40 years since I applied for membership of the Prague Musical Society "Cecilie", which was directed by the experienced conductor, A. Apt, who did much to raise musical standards in Prague at that time. I joined the "Cecilie" orchestra as a viola player. "You will play at the same desk as Dvořák," said Apt, and introduced me to a young man with a mane of typically tousled, thick black hair. We were both young men of barely twenty years. Dvořák was a pupil of the Organ-school directed by the pedagogue, Josef Krejčí, with whom I studied privately. So I began to play with Dvořák, but I can tell you it was no easy matter. Now my playing did not please him, now he was annoyed with the next desk, another time he was dissatisfied with the conductor—or with himself. And now and again he would stop playing and start humming some scrap of melody to himself.

"Cecilie" was dissolved after being in existence for 25 years and we did not come together again till November 1862 in the orchestra of the Prozatímní Divadlo (Interim Theatre), where he was first viola and I was choir-master. Dvořák had then already begun to compose smaller pieces—songs and musical entractes.

From the book "From my Memories of the Theatre" by *Adolf Čech* (1841-1903), for long years conductor in succession to Bedřich Smetana at the National Theatre in Prague.—The St. Cecilie Union, the Prague Choral and Musical Society, founded in, and conducted from, the year 1840 by the musical amateur, Antonín Apt (1815-1887), an enthusiastic admirer of Romantic music. The society was dissolved at the beginning of 1860.—Dvořák composed at that time not only songs (the cycle "The Cypresses" in 1865) and entractes, but also chamber music, two symphonies (C minor and B flat major) and other works.

10. DVOŘÁK'S MUSICAL BEGINNINGS

... Later a composer of world renown, professor at the Prague Conservatoire, then director of the New York and later of the Prague Conservatoire, he enjoyed talking in the intimate circle of his friends, and with irresistable humour, of his "performances" in his first calling of butcher, of the enthusiastic ado with which the public greeted the Hungarian Dances, long before their artistic arrangement by Brahms, as played by the band of which Dvořák was a member up to the time he and the band were taken over by the Prozatimní Theatre, or he would relate how, as organist of St. Catherine's, he improved his knowledge of the other official language of the country with the help of a harmless idiot who blew the organ-bellows for him. This period of Dvořák's life has not a little of the Bohemian flavour, and this Bohemianism is, I should say, more democratic than artistic—a Bohemianism which possibly explains why Dvořák, in later years, found relaxation in the popular atmosphere of a beer-restaurant rather than in the most brilliant salons, or that in later years, too, he could enter into the spirit and fully appreciate the performance of a "tavern sextet", a musical institution which, for the present generation, is gradually becoming a thing unknown, but one that, especially on summer evenings, is not without a certain charm of its own...

From "*Recollections of Antonín Dvořák*" by *Joseph Zubatý* (see 8). After completing his studies at the Organ-school, Dvořák played viola in the popular Prague band of Karel Komzák, which in 1862 became the orchestra of the then newly opened "Prozatímní" theatre (see 12). *Karel Komzák*, popular composer of dance pieces and, later, Austrian regimental bandmaster, also acted as organist in the Prague Institute for Mental Cases where Dvořák sometimes played for him.

11. RECOLLECTIONS OF DVOŘÁK'S FAMILY LIFE

Dvořák boarded with us alone as we had only one room and a kitchen. Very soon, however, he had to find some source of earnings as Uncle, his Father, was not doing at all well, especially after the move to Kladno, and could not give him anything. Antonín had breakfast with us and went to an eating-place near the National Theatre for dinner and supper. His mother saw to his laundry. In the plum season he would ask Mother to give him dinner and I still see Mother, in my mind's eye, counting 30 plum dumplings on to a dish for Antonín—of which not one remained! For a time he had supper at home, too.

Then Mother, who was the life and soul of our household, rented a larger flat, with two rooms and a kitchen, in the same house so that she could earn something by taking in lodgers and from then on Dvořák shared the room with another lodger—a student.

When we moved to "na Křemelci", our third move, to a flat in the back annex to a house with a garden, Dvořák lived in a nice three-windowed room with two other lodgers. He had a piano hired from his tailor at 2 gulden a month, a table opposite it and behind it his bed. He often composed immediately on waking—in bed, and whenever he got an idea, he played it over—on the eiderdown. When he used to write at the table, he held the quill in his teeth and played with his fingers on his jacket or on his legs. After a while he went to the piano and played it over, singing softly at the same time. When he played in the orchestra of the Interim Theatre, he often took me with him to the performance. I used to sit on a chair in the orchestra, and never had to be reprimanded twice. I sat there, scarcely breathing, just taking in all the beauty in great gasps. Often when he was playing the piano I would creep into the room, go up to the piano, and beg him for whole quarters-of-an-hour at a time: "Anton, please take me with you, today, please take me!" He would fix his eyes on mine, smile, whistle under his breath, quite unaware, I am sure, of my existence. And then, on coming down to earth again, he would sudddenly exclaim: "What do you want?" making me jump with the start he gave me.

My parents were pious folks and said their prayers morning and evening kneeling. Mother invited young Dvořák to join them: "Auntie, I like praying best there at the window when I look out on to the green and at the sky." I never heard my cousin speak vulgarly, flippantly or indelicately. He was through and through of noble character, of high morals and his conduct was without reproach. He never came home late, he had no female acquaintances and no love affairs, and in our family they used to say that "Anton was afraid of women". I remember him saying on occasion: "That's a pretty girl!" but that was as far as he went. Once the young people of two or three neighbouring families arranged a fancy-dress party at our place because we had a piano. They asked Dvořák to join them and play for them; but he did not come home at all that night and slept somewhere else for the first time.

In 1864 Dvořák went for the third time to the military call-up and all supposed that the strong young man who had never had a serious illness would not come back. We had bewailed his going as if it were a fact and all the greater was then our joy when—he was not accepted.

From Anna Dušková's "Recollections of Antonín Dvořák" (see 5).

12. DVOŘÁK IN THE ORCHESTRA OF THE CZECH THEATRE.

By a fortunate chance, walking along the Charles Square in Prague, I met Mr. Kváča, the only musician still alive of the band that was taken over in 1862 by the Czech Interim theatre. This is what he related:

Dvořák was easily roused, quick-tempered and impatient and used to avoid those colleagues who liked to raise his ire, and then he played the solo parts on the viola d'amour in "Der Freischütz" and in "Les Huguenots" very well.

He was too poor to have his own piano and so he went to Kváča's flat to play over his things. This Mrs. Kváča did not particularly welcome as he always left his footmarks on the newly-scrubbed floor. So he took a room where there was a piano at his disposal, but sometimes he took too great advantage of it for, when some idea occurred to him in the night, he got up and played it over so as not to forget it, without considering that the other people in the flat were asleep. This was the main reason for his frequent changes of rooms. And also when he lived together with Anger, he would often monopolize his piano the whole day.

Extract from a letter by Petr Mareš. Petr Mareš and *Jan Kváča*, members of the orchestra of the Prague Interim theatre in which Dvořák also played viola in the years 1862-1871.—*Mořic Anger* (1844-1905), at first violinist in, and then second conductor of, the Czech Theatre orchestra in Prague.

13. DVOŘÁK AS ORGANIST (I)

Ref. no. 12,327.—The Town Council herewith appoints to the post of organist to the parish church of St. Adalbert, Antonín Dvořák, teacher of music and composer, resident in no. 27 "na Florenci", on condition that he should personally and satisfactorily fill this post, and, at the same time, calls upon him to take up his duties as from February 15th of the current year, to which end he should report at the parish office.

The Town Council hereby informs the parish office of this in an appendix to the decree dated 13. January 1874, no. 996, and directs the said office to take Antonín Dvořák into their service and to report immediately on their having done so in order that the emolument due to him may be paid out.

The Town Council in Prague, 10th February 1874.

Burgomaster: Jos. Hulesch m. p.

In the years 1874-1877 Dvořák held the appointment of organist to the church of St. Adalbert at a yearly salary of 126 gulden.

14. DVOŘÁK AS ORGANIST (II)

The tiny chancel of St Adalbert's. A bunch of singers—ladies and gentlemen—fill it. Josef Foerster, with his goatee, conducting, stands close to the rail. To catch a glimpse of Antonín Dvořák on the organ-bench is difficult. He improvises with restraint: Stehle, Witt, had also written—or so it would seem—the preludes to their masses: so closely did Dvořák keep to their style in introducing them...

Leoš Janáček: "Recollections of Antonín Dvořák."—The well-known Czech composer, Leoš Janáček (1854-1928), the author of the internationally famous opera "Jenufa" and other operas and compositions, entered into a very warm friendship with Dvořák during his studies at the Prague Organ-School. He was a very zealous propagator of Dvořák's compositions especially as conductor of the Philharmonic Society in Brno in Moravia.—Director of the choir at St. Adalbert's was, at that time, the composer and theoretician, Prof. Josef Foerster (1833-1907), father of the composer Josef Bohuslav Foerster (see 15).—Ed. J. G. Stehle, F. Witt, well-known German composers for the organ.

15. DVOŘÁK AS ORGANIST (III)

...We met every Sunday and every church feast day: Antonín Dvořák, organist of St. Adalbert's in Jircháři, and I, chorister in the same church. When I and the other boys were putting the music on the desks, renewing strings that had burst, putting resin on the bows and hanging up the horns and trumpets on the nails beside the desks, Antonín Dvořák regularly came in. He paid no heed to anybody, greeted nobody and sat down straight away at the organ. The organ-bench of the old instrument was placed at the side, the organist having to follow the conductor's beat in a mirror above the keyboard and so he sat with his back to the choir, the conductor and all those taking part. For that reason I seldom saw Dvořák's face but I recollect how, as a child, the severe expression of his countenance and the unvaryingly serious appearance of this man, always deep in his own strange thoughts, made me feel afraid.

I have already said that nobody had any idea how great an artist filled the humble post of organist at St. Adalbert's. Dvořák's improvisation was without doubt correct as regards harmony and by no means common-place, but did not warrant his being looked upon as an exceptional talent. I, myself, however, was not capable of criticizing the Master's playing, but I know that my Father, who was director of the choral music at St. Adalbert's, often spoke of it in this sense...

At that time nobody knew that the poor organist of St. Adalbert's, with a monthly salary of 10 gulden, might be found sitting at his table, in the rare intervals of his leisure, working hard at a big opera, still less did they guess that he had a number of scores at home, among them the "Hymnus", to words by Hálek, and that work of genius—"Stabat Mater" which, some years later, was to make him famous throughout the whole cultured world.

Josef Boh. Foerster: "Recollections of the organist at St. Adalbert's." *Foerster* (1859-1951), one of the foremost of Czech composers, later President of the Czech Academy of Sciences and Arts and National Artist, son of the choir director, Josef Foerster sen. (see 16).—The "*Hymnus*" see 16.—*Stabat Mater* for solo voices, mixed choir and orchestra was not written by Dvořák till the years 1876-77 when he was no longer organist.

16. DVOŘÁK'S FIRST SUCCESS AS A COMPOSER

On the 9th March 1873, "Hlahol" held an extraordinary concert in the New Town Theatre at which, in addition to a male choir and orchestra, a choir of 90 ladies appeared for the first time... This concert was remarkable also for the rare novelties included in the programme, of which the greatest success was achieved by the magnificent "Hymnus" of Antonín Dvořák.

1. Nelahozeves, Antonín Dvořák's native village (contemporary engraving).

2. The family house and birthplace of Antonín Dvořák in Nelahozeves.

As one of the reporters expressed it: "It carried the whole audience off its feet on a wave of enthusiasm and can, with full justice, be described as the most brilliant item on the programme..."

Chronicle of the Prague choral union "Hlahol". The Hymnus, op. 30, for mixed choir and orchestra, to words from the poem "The Heirs of the White Mountain", by Vítězslav Hálek, was finished on the 3rd June 1872. It is a composition with an ardently patriotic theme, actively directed against the age-long oppression of the Czech nation by the Austrian dynasty and one to which Dvořák succeeded in giving appropriate musical expression. Its first performance at the concert given by "Hlahol" signified a decided success for Dvořák among the Prague musical public. The composition was conducted by the composer and choir-master, Karel Bendl (1836-1896), from his youth Dvořák's good friend, who helped him at the beginning of his career by lending him music and a piano.

17. THE FIRST FAILURE AND SUCCESS OF DVOŘÁK'S DRAMATIC MUSIC

... But once there was great excitement in the choir of St. Adalbert's. One of the members of the choir, who was at the same time a member of the Czech opera, brought the news: Dvořák has handed in an opera. It seemed almost unbelievable but nobody had the courage to ask the presumed author. Shortly afterwards a notice appeared in the daily press. It was really true. Antonín Dvořák had presented the Czech theatre with an opera in three acts *"King and Charcoal Burner"*.

It was a long time, I can still remember, before they began to study the work, or at least it seemed so to us who were very curious to know what Dvořák's opera music would be like. At last the time came but the answer we got was not satisfactory. Nothing about whether the music was good, characteristic, suited to the theme or whether it had dramatic verve. Nor did the news improve–till one day things came to a head and there befell a catastrophe which would have spelt defeat for any merely

33

average talent. The theatre returned the score to the composer...

I do not know how Antonín Dvořák took this heavy blow of fate, I only remember that we were all very sorry for him. Without having any proper idea of the severe spiritual and nervous strain which is required to produce a 3-act opera, quite apart from the immense physical labour, we yet felt sincere sympathy for the poor, silent organist in whom we sensed a being different from the common run, but essentially good.

And even then Dvořák showed all those who had eyes to see his uncommon greatness. The critical moment found him strong and resistant to the hardest blows of fate. Though depressed by family troubles, he did not lose courage. He consigned the rejected score to the flames of his poor man's fire and—began to write again. In less than a year, I think, he submitted to the theatre a new version of "King and Charcoal-Burner". And then it was not only rehearsed but also produced.

In the choir of St. Adalbert's the reports grew more favourable from Sunday to Sunday, and the more the work on it progressed, the greater was the appreciation and admiration—people talked of the surprising wealth of melodic beauty, of the dramatic tension of the principal scenes, of the splendid handling of the themes and polyphony. And when the first performance was over, we all knew that in Antonín Dvořák there was growing up for Czech art one of the rarest of the rare, an artist called and chosen...

Josef B. Foerster (see 15): *"Recollections of the Organist of St. Adalbert's."*—The opera *"King and Charcoal-Burner"*, the second of Dvořák's musico-dramatic works, of whose failure Foerster here speaks, was written in 1871. The report that Dvořák destroyed this opera proved to be erroneous, for it was found long after the composer's death and produced at the National Theatre in Prague on May 28th 1929. The completely new musical rendering of the same libretto from the first version of which not a single bar was taken over, was written in 1874 and its first performance took place at the Prague Interim theatre on the 24th November 1874.—The plot of the opera is the relatively naively handled story of a Czech King of long ago who when hunting lost his way in the deep forest where he made the acquaintance of a poor charcoal-burner's family. He did not reveal himself till his return to the Prague Castle to which he invited them on learning that unknowingly he had caused dissension between the charcoal-burner's daughter and her jealous lover.

18. A STATE GRANT

To the Town Clerk.

Dear Sir, I should be obliged if you would be good enough to furnish me with a certificate in German confirming that I am without means, as such a certificate must be enclosed with my application for the award of a State grant for artists, such application to be sent in by the 30th instant at the latest.

Prague, 15th June 1874.

Ant. Dvořák m. p.

Certificate confirming that Antonín Dvořák, teacher of music, resident at no. 1364, is without means.

The Town Clerk's Office of the Royal Capital of Prague hereby confirms, for the purpose of gaining a State grant, due official investigation having been made, that Antonín Dvořák, teacher of music, born in 1841, married and father of one unprovided child, has no property, and that, except for a salary of 126 gulden which he receives as organist of the Church of St. Adalbert and 60 gulden which he earns monthly by the private teaching of music, he has no other source of income.

Prague, 24. 6. 1874.

Elk m. p.

In 1874 Dvořák sent in his first application for an Austrian State grant which the Ministry of Education at that time awarded every year to "young, poor and talented artists" (poets, artists and musicians). Adviser to the Musical Department of the Ministry was the musical theoretician and, for many years, musical critic of the Vienna daily "Die Neue Freie Presse", Dr. Ed. Hanslick (1825-1904); other members of the adjudicating board were *Johannes Brahms*, then shortly afterwards, Dvořák's loyal friend and director of the Vienna Hofoper, *Johann Herbeck* (1833-1877). Dvořák received the grant for five years in succession and it was a very welcome contribution to the upkeep of the poor household he had founded on his marriage, at the end of 1873, to *Anna Čermáková*, the daughter of a Prague goldsmith and a very efficient alto. The first three children of this marriage, a son and two daughters, died in early infancy.

19. FIRST STEPS TO WORLD SUCCESS

... Many years ago, when Dvořák was at the beginning of his career, Mr. Kaván brought Dvořák to our house, wishing, as he said, to recommend "a young and talented musician" as his successor in teaching pianoforte in our family. We then spent many an agreeable evening playing and singing. We were specially fond of vocal duets which Dvořák obligingly accompanied. Only the limited choice annoyed us not a little. We got tired of the hackneyed repetition of Mendelssohn and other German composers. My husband, an ardent Moravian, once remarked to Dvořák in passing: "Wouldn't it be possible to compose some duets from our own music, for instance from Moravian folk-songs?" "Why not?"–replied Dvořák. "Look out some nice texts and I shall do the rest." No sooner said than done. Our governess borrowed Sušil's Collection and made her own selection of about 15 songs. Dvořák promised to write a second part for them and a piano accompaniment. In a few days, however, he announced that he had changed his mind. "I won't do that," he said, "if you like I'll write duets in my own way but I won't write a second part for these things." Nobody had any objection and Dvořák set to work according to his own ideas and composed his famous "Moravian Duets". He dedicated them to me and to my husband as a token of our friendship.

When I went over them for the first time and praised them, the young composer sighed: "A pity I haven't the wherewithal. I'd like to have them published." Whereupon my husband's immediate rejoinder was: "Now wait a bit, I shall see about getting them published, and, if you agree, half the edition will be yours and half mine, and we shall each be free to do what we like with our copies." Dvořák gladly agreed. The Moravian Duets were lithographed at Starý's, a number of copies we kept for ourselves and for our friends while Dvořák received the remainder. Once, in his absence, it was decided to have a number of copies exquisitely bound and sent to the most outstanding musicians, musical critics and patriotic Czech personalities. We did so without asking Dvořák as we knew that he would not want to give his consent... The Duets were sent to Brahms and Hanslick, a man whose word carried the greatest weight in our part of the musical world, while the Slavonic world was represented by Bishop Strossmayer and others. Strossmayer received the Duets with a patriotic note, Brahms and Hanslick with the respectful request that they might accept them and give their criticism. And all this without the slightest inkling on the part of our unsuspecting composer...

A reminiscence by Marie Neffová, wife of the Prague businessman, Jan Neff, a native of Moravia, a great lover of music and singing and a generous patron of Moravian students.—The famous *Moravian Duets*, composed on texts of folk-poetry, were written as op. 32 between May and July 1876. The texts were taken from the comprehensive and admirable collection of "Moravian National Songs with Music and Texts" which was compiled and published by the Moravian priest and collector, *František Sušil*, in 1860. The Moravian Duets were published by F. Simrock of Berlin at the beginning of 1878 as Dvořák's first work to be published by this big firm of music publishers. It was these Duets which, as the fruit of a peculiarly individual stylisation, typically folk-art in spirit yet realized with the expressive means of art music, founded the reputation of the Czech composer also abroad.—*Emanuel Starý*, the founder of the first Czech music publishing firm.—*Bishop Josip Strossmayer*, an outstanding leader of the Croatian national movement and friend of the Czech nation (1815-1905).

20. DVOŘÁK GIVES UP HIS POST AS ORGANIST

Ref. no. 134, 724.—Mr. Antonín Dvořák, organist to the church of St. Adalbert, has informed the Town Council that he is giving up this post and asks to be relieved, at his own request, of his duties as from 15th February 1877. The Town Council accept his resignation and direct the parish office to cease making payment of salary to the above-named organist as from 15th February 1877.

The Town Council of Prague, 2nd January 1877.

Burgomaster: Em. Skramlík m. p.

21. THE BEGINNINGS OF A FRIENDSHIP

Prague 3. 12. 77. Žitnobranská 10. II.

Honoured Sir,

I have lately received a letter from the esteemed Prof. Dr. Hanslick in which he informs me that at a recent session with His Excellency, Minister Stremayer, I was, on your kind recommendation and that of the Professor, awarded a grant for artists.

At the suggestion of the esteemed Prof. Hanslick, I venture to address these few lines to you, honoured Master, in order to express to you my deep-felt thanks for the kindness you have shown me.

What I count a still greater happiness, however, is the sympathy you have been good enough to accord to my modest talent and the favour with which (as Prof. Hanslick tells me) you received my Czech vocal duets. Prof. Hanslick now advises me to procure a German translation of these songs which you, dear Sir, would be so kind as to recommend to your publisher. It is my duty to address myself to you with one more request—that you should be good enough to be of assistance to me in this matter which, for me, is of such great importance. It would be, indeed, not only for me but also for my beloved country, of immeasurable value if you, honoured Master, whose works delight in such great measure the whole musical world, would give me such an introduction.

With the earnest request that I may continue in the future to enjoy your highly valued favour, I beg your kind permission to forward to you for your inspection some of my chamber music works and compositions for orchestra.

I have the honour to be,

Your most respectful and devoted

Antonín Dvořák.

Dvořák to Brahms in Vienna.—For note on Brahms and Hanslick see 18.— *Karel Stremayer*, 1870-1879 Austrian Minister of Education.—The two-part Czech songs referred to here are the Moravian Duets, see 19.—Brahm's publisher: Fritz Simrock (see 19 and 22-23).

38

22. BRAHMS'S FIRST REPLY

Dear Sir,

Allow me quite shortly to thank you for your lines and for the great pleasure I have derived from the works you sent me. I have taken the liberty of writing about them, and especially about the "Duets", to Mr. Fritz Simrock (Berlin, W. Friedrichstrasse 171).

From the title it would appear that the Duets are still your property, in which case you could sell them to Mr. Simrock. The only thing that is needed is to get a good German translation. Can you manage that? In any case I beg you not to rush the matter so that the work may not suffer in consequence. In the meantime you could perhaps send the folio to Mr. Simrock to have a look at? The rest will then follow.

Forgive my being in haste today but I should not like to have the matter delayed. Hoping to hear further from you and favourably,

I remain,
Your very respectful and entirely devoted
J. Brahms.

Vienna IV, Karlgasse 9.

Brahms to Dvořák in Prague, December 1877.—*Fritz Simrock* (1837-1901), in the years 1864-1901 proprietor and head of the big music-publishing firm in Berlin, now no longer in existence. He was the publisher of Brahm's works and Dvořák's principal publisher.—On the publication of the Moravian Duets by Simrock see 19.

23. BRAHMS RECOMMENDS DVOŘÁK TO SIMROCK

Dear S.

In connection with the State grant, I have for several years past had great pleasure in the works of Antonín *Dvořák* (pronounce Dworschak) in Prague. This year he sent in, among other things, a volume (10) of "Duets for 2 sopranos with piano accompaniment", which seems to be very suitable and *practical* for publication. The volume appears to have been printed at the composer's own expense. The title and, unfortunately, also the texts are in Czech only. I have advised him to send you the songs. When you play them over you will be, like I was, delighted, and as a publisher you will be particularly delighted with their piquant charm. It would be necessary, however, to really see to getting a very good translation. Now there are quite a number of texts translated by Wenzig (who died a short time ago). Failing that there is Dr. Siegfried *Kapper* in Prague, who might be suitable for the purpose. Dvořák has written all sorts of things, operas (Czech), symphonies, quartets and piano music. There is no doubt he is very talented. And then he is also poor. I beg you to think the matter over. The "Duets" won't give you much thought and will possibly sell well. The address is: Praha, Žitná ulice no. 10, II...

> With best greetings,
> > Yours,
> > > > J. Br.

Brahms in Vienna to Simrock in Berlin, 12. XII. 1877.—See preceding letter.—Dvořák lived in no. 10 Žitná ulice (Praha II, 564) from 1877 till the artist's death in 1904.

24. DVOŘÁK THANKS BRAHMS

Praha, 19. 12. 77.
Žitná ul. 10/II.

Honoured Master,

I beg you to accept my apologies for not having been able to thank you sooner for your highly esteemed letter which I received late owing to my absence for some days from Prague.

Allow me, dear Sir, to express once again my most humble thanks for all that you have done for me.

As regards the German translation of my songs, I am glad to be able to inform you that it is already completed. I therefore take the liberty of sending you a copy for your kind inspection. I have also sent a copy to Mr. Simrock.

As soon as I have any further news, I shall not fail to communicate with you.

May this letter of mine be an auspicious one and may I soon have the pleasure of assuring you personally how sincerely I am,

Your deeply obliged and most devoted servant,

Antonín Dvořák.

The Moravian Duets were translated by the Czech composer, Josef Srb-Debrnov (1836-1904).

25. DVOŘÁK DEDICATES HIS QUARTET TO BRAHMS

Praha, 23. 1. 78.

Honoured Master,

About three weeks ago I set out on my intended journey to Vienna in order to thank you personally for all the kindness you have shown me. I was very sorry that I was not fortunate enough to see you before you left for Leipzig. I took the opportunity to visit Prof. Hanslick who received me very cordially. At his request I left a number of my compositions with your housekeeper and beg you, if you are already back in Vienna, to be so good as to look them through. At the same time I take the liberty of inquiring whether you received the Duets with the German translation and whether it is good.

Mr. Simrock wrote to me a few days ago. He will be pleased to publish the Duets, only a number of places must be changed for the sake of declamation.

I have further the honour to inform you that your splendid
D minor Concerto was performed at a concert given recently
here in Prague and was extremely successful.

And now I venture, highly honoured Master, to approach
you with a request. Permit me, out of gratitude and a deep respect for your incomparable musical works, to offer you the
dedication of my D minor Quartet.

It would be for me the highest honour I can aspire to and
I should be the happiest of men to have the honour to subscribe
myself as bound to you in eternal gratitude and

Your devoted Servant,

Antonín Dvořák.

At the beginning of January 1878, Brahms left Vienna on a concert tour of a
number of German towns (Leipzig, Hamburg, Bremen) and of Holland, where for the
most part he conducted his first Symphony in C minor or what was his second and new
Symphony in D major.—Dvořák dedicated to him his *String Quartet in D minor*,
op. 34, composed between the 7th and 18th of December 1877.

26. BRAHMS ACCEPTS THE DEDICATION

Dear Sir,

I regret extremely that I was away from home when you
were here. The more so as I have such an aversion to letter-
writing that I cannot hope to make up for it in the least by
correspondence. And, today, no more than to say that to occupy
myself with your things gives me the greatest pleasure, but that
I would give a good deal to be able to discuss individual points
with you personally. You write somewhat hurriedly. When you
are filling in the numerous missing sharps, flats and naturals,
then it would be good to look a little more closely at the notes
themselves and at the voice parts etc.

Forgive me, but it is very desirable to point out such things
to a man like you. I also accept the works just as they are very

gratefully and consider myself honoured by the dedication of the quartet.

I think it would be very good if you gave me both the quartets that I know. If Simrock should not be willing, might I try to place them elsewhere?

Accept once more my best thanks for your news
and warm greetings from
Your entirely devoted

J. Brahms.

Brahms in Vienna to Dvořák in Prague, III. 1878.—See preceding letter. The two well-known quartets: E major op. 27 from the year 1876, published later by Simrock as op. 80, and the D minor quartet, op. 34, which was published by Schlesinger in Berlin.

27. BRAHMS RENEWS HIS RECOMMENDATION

Dear S.

I am leaving within the next few days with *Billroth* and *Goldmark* for Italy. I shall probably stop in Pörtschach am See —if it is too hot in Italy. I should not have written if it had not been for thinking of *Dvořák*.

I don't know what further risk you are wanting to take with this man. I have no idea about business matters or what interest there is for larger works. I do not care to make recommendations, because I have only my eyes and my ears and they are altogether my own. If you should think of going on with it at all, get him to send you his two string quartets, major and minor, and have them played to you. The best that a musician can have *Dvořák has*, and it is in these compositions. I am an incorrigible philistine—I should publish even my own works for the pleasure of it.

In short I cannot say anything more than that I recommend Dvořák in general and in particular. Besides you have your own ears and business sense to guide you...

　　With kind regards and greetings,
　　　　　　Yours

J. Br.

Brahms in Vienna to Simrock in Berlin, 5. IV. 1878. *Prof. Dr. Christian Billroth* (1829-1894), the famous Viennese surgeon, an enthusiastic lover of music and Brahms's devoted friend.—*Karl Goldmark* (1830-1915), German composer, author of the repertoire opera "The Queen of Sheba". The two quartets, major and minor: see 26.

28. NERUDA AND "THE PEASANT A ROGUE"

Antonín Dvořák.

Here we present to you the father of "The Peasant a Rogue". He is father a number of times over, but of all his children so far we like "The Peasant a Rogue" best. A strapping youth with sparkling eyes, a springy step and always a song on his lips. And if we wanted to tell you what the songs are like, we should again have to make use of a peasant anecdote about the peasant who was at the Opera for the first time. "One of them sang so badly that she had to repeat everything twice."— The songs in Dvořák's operas are also so "bad" that the unsatisfied audience always has them repeated twice. "God above, give us more like 'em!" we called out when we heard them for the first time. It is true, art is not "bread" but it is the wine of human life—our Czech life needs a good draught of health-giving wine.

　　I do not know Dvořák personally or what he is like, but I imagine him a real musician. That is "a poet of the air" as they call musicians who care not a fig about what is going on down here on the earth far beneath them. A creature who is mightily indifferent as to whether a heller and a groschen are all that he has left in his pocket. A young man with the conf-

44

used brain which is attributed to every poet, to every painter and most of all to the musical tribe all the world over. What would there be special about him if he was altogether sensible and—everyday.

Just as it is sometimes accounted a fault in a lovely young lady that she is "too" young—it is a fault which (you may be sure) time will remedy. He is also said to be "ambitious". Bravo! I could embrace him for that! And then that he works too much. Let us reproach the ocean that it has "too many" waves. Once there was a musician and his name was Beethoven. He is said to have written a great deal, a very deal great. And when he was lying on his death-bed, he said: "It seems to me as if I were only at the beginning". May it always seem to Dvořák as if he were only at the beginning!

Jan Neruda (1834-1891), a celebrated Czech poet, publicist and critic, the creator of the Czech essay and the Czech feuilleton. An enthusiastic notice of a jokingly playful character accompanied Dvořák's portrait in the Czech "Humoristické listy" (a satiric illustrated magazine) after the première of the comic two-act opera "The Peasant a Rogue". In this opera a wealthy farmer has sought out a bridegroom for his daughter and so opposes her love for a poor youth. Unknowingly the reigning Prince saves the lovers when his own wife discovers him making love to the girl.—The opera was first performed on the 27th January 1878 at the Czech Theatre in Prague and was published by Simrock, Berlin. Regarding its production on several German stages see 61, and 62.

29. DVOŘÁK'S FIRST AUTHOR'S FEE

When I first had the opportunity to come into personal contact with Dvořák, he had already risen above the worst hardships. He was no longer dependent on ways of earning a livelihood which robbed him of so much time—time that he would gladly and with such advantage have devoted to his proper work of composing. All the same he was still far from being a "well-situated" artist, for his chief source of income at that time was the State grant for artists which he had received for a number of years and for which thanks were chiefly due to Brahms as the then advisor to the Minister of Education in Vienna. But he was an artist whose name was cropping up ever more frequently in the Prague musical chronicle, who was preparing—again thanks to Brahms—to make his first steps abroad, who could even at last afford the luxury of having a piano at home—not his own, to be sure, but on hire. And this existence, such as the State grant made possible, but which had still to be supplemented by the fee from some better-paid music lesson, could only seem to be the beginning of prosperity for a man so little pampered by fortune as was Dvořák. How modest were at that time the claims that Dvořák made on life as the recompense for so many years of striving and hardship, for so many years of work devoted to his art, is perhaps best illustrated by one small incident. I shall not easily forget with what triumph Dvořák, in 1878, brought to the usual afternoon meeting at our café an envelope in which he had been sent for the first series of Slavonic Dances the first fee (or first decent fee) he received for published work; it was, if I am not mistaken, 200 or 250 marks.

Dr. Josef Zubatý (see 8): "Recollection of Ant. Dvořák." — For the first series of eight piano duets, entitled "Slavonic Dances" op. 46, which was composed between March and the 7th May 1878 and soon laid the foundations of the composer's fame throughout the world, Dvořák received from Simrock the fee of 300 German marks!

30. LOUIS EHLERT "DISCOVERS" DVOŘÁK

...I was sitting one day in very had humour buried in a heap of musical novelties, eye and spirit struggling with the faintness which so easily overcomes us under the impression of empty, indifferent, in short, insignificant music when suddenly two works, by a composer so far unknown to me, engrossed all my attention: "Slavonic Dances" for four hands and "Moravian Songs", 13 duets for soprano and contralto, by Antonín Dvořák.

The composer is a Czech, lives in Prague and was, up till a few years ago, viola player in the Opera there. He has as yet published very few things, but he is said to have a large number of compositions ready including quartets and symphonies. This is all I could find out about him. To put the matter shortly: Here at last is a hundred per cent talent and, what is more, a completely natural talent. I consider the Slavonic Dances to be a work which will make its triumphant way through the world in the same way as Brahms's Hungarian Dances. There is no question here of some kind of imitation; his dances are not in the least Brahmsian. Divine Providence flows through this music and that is why it is altogether popular. Not a trace of artificiality or constraint. They could be scored straight away, everything is so effectively and colourfully arranged. To what extent and what material has been taken over into these compositions from Czech folk music I do not know; it is also immaterial. Who asks on seeing Shakespeare's plays on what old Welsh tale, or on hearing Schubert's Divertissement a l'hongroise, on what Hungarian song, the one or other is based? Here we are confronted with perfected works of art and not perhaps with some pastiche stuck together from scraps of national melody. As always among talents of a high order, humour has an important place in Dvořák's music. Dvořák writes such jolly basses that the heart of every musician worth the name must laugh within him. The duets, based on very charming folk-verses, are also remarkable for their delightful freshness. On reading them I felt in my heart as if I were watching lovely girls pelting each other with sweet-scented flowers on which the dew was still sparkling. I do not say that what we have here is genius, for that we must await further works, but undoubtedly we have before us a very pleasing talent. And that is what we are much in need of. The men who awaken at the present time the greatest interest in the sphere of music are so terribly serious. I cannot help thinking how splendid it would be if a musician should appear once again whom we should as little think of quarrelling about as

47

about Spring. Whoever finds a jewel on the public highway is under obligation to report his find. I beg the reader to look upon these lines from that point of view—and from yet another. Anyone who knows how difficult it is to draw the attention of the public to an artist who has not yet made a name for himself, should, as far as it is within his power, awaken and encourage this attention. For, just as all advertisement is repugnant, so every effort is justified which aims at shortening the gloomy period of obscurity for real talents.

Louis Ehlert (1825-1884), German writer on music and composer, music critic of "Die Neue Musikzeitung" in Berlin, lived from 1873 in Wiesbaden. His enthusiastic notice, published in the "Nationalzeitung", helped Dvořák to rapid recognition in Germany. Dvořák out of gratitude dedicated to him his Serenade for Wind Instruments in D minor, op. 44, which he composed in January 1878.

31. LOUIS EHLERT TO DVOŘÁK

Wiesbaden 27/11 78
10, Frankfurter Str.

Dear Sir,

I knew very well that my notice in the Nationalzeitung would give you pleasure and be of service to you, but all the same I was pleasently touched that you should confirm it...

In Berlin my critique produced a positive "run" on the music shops and, I can say without exaggeration, made you a name over night. Heaven grant that the high opinion I have of your talent may be fully confirmed.

In me you will always find a man who will back the fulfilment of this hope with his whole, if inconsiderable, influence.

If you have a picture of yourself, send it to me. One likes to know what the person in whom he takes an interest looks like.

With kind regards,

I am, Yours very sincerely,

Louis Ehlert.

See 30.

3. Facsimile of a page from the manuscript of the first String Quartet in A major.

4. Antonín Dvořák (c. 1872).

32. BEDŘICH SMETANA ON DVOŘÁK

...At the time the score of the Slavonic Dances was being published in Berlin, Smetana happened to be in Prague and was staying, as always, with his devoted friend, J. Srb-Debrnov in Jirchǎři. Smetana expressed sincere pleasure at our Czech music making an impression abroad but at the same time indicated his regret that he did not know the things and remarked that "the young composers should at least show old Smetana their published work" even though he could no longer hear it. His wish was granted through the kind offices of his friend Srb and the next day Smetana was able to look through the score of the Slavonic Dances. I was present when Smetana unreservedly praised the work: among other things he said that in this work Dvořák handled his themes "in a truly Beethoven-like manner".

From an article by the noted Czech zoologist, *Dr. František Bayer* (1854-1936).— *Bedřich Smetana* (1824-1884), the founder of modern Czech music and author of the world-famed opera "The Bartered Bride".—Slavonic Dances see 29.—Srb-Debrnov see 24.

33. DVOŘÁK'S FIRST VISIT TO BERLIN

Dear Friend,

I arrived in Berlin on Tuesday and went straight to Simrock who was expecting me. I had not been here more than a few hours before I had spent among the foremost artists so many happy and agreeable moments that the memory of them will remain with me for the rest of my life.

Joachim had been looking forward eagerly to my arrival and held a soirée for me at 7 p. m. at which my new quartet and sextet were performed. How they played everything and with what understanding and enthusiasm, I cannot tell you now. But

I shall tell you all about it when I come to see you again at Sichrov. That will be on Saturday without fail.

Goodbye for the present,

Yours,

Ant. Dvořák.

Dvořák to Alois Göbl. Göbl (1841-1907), secretary on the estate of Prince Rohan in Sychrov by Turnov in Bohemia, an excellent singer and Dvořák's very intimate friend from the time of his membership of the Interim Theatre orchestra till the artist's death.—*Josef Joachim*, director of the Musikhochschule in Berlin, a famous violinist who often gave concerts in England and leader of his own Quartet, with which he gave first performances of Dvořák's *Sextet in A major*, op. 48 (from the year 1878) and *Quartet in E flat major*, op. 51 (1879) in Germany and England.

34. EHLERT ON THE SEXTET AND QUARTET

Wiesbaden 19/10 79

24, Frankfurter Str.

Dear Sir,

Just a word to tell you that in your Sextet and Quartet I have found works such as I would always wish to have from you. They are masterly compositions worthy of the highest respect. Friend Rebicek would like to perform them here and I can tell you even now with prophetic certainty that they will go round the world.

I felt I must say this to you and, at the same time, assure you of the great pleasure it gives me to do so.

Yours sincerely,

Louis Ehlert.

Your III. Rhapsody is being performed here today, at my request. The rest of them later.

Louis Ehlert to Dvořák in Prague (see 30).—*Josef Řebiček (Rebicek)*, violinist, graduate of the Prague Conservatoire, at this time leader of the Hoftheater orchestra in Wiesbaden where he was later Kapellmeister and from 1897-1903 conductor of the Philharmonic Orchestra in Berlin.—*III. Slavonic Rhapsody* (op. 45 no. 3), composed at the end of 1878.

35. DVOŘÁK WELCOMES BRAHMS'S CRITICISM

Honoured Master,   Prague, 15. X. 79.

During your last stay in Prague you were so kind as to draw my attention to a number of things in my works and I must be very grateful to you for it as I have since found many bad notes which I have put right.

I found myself obliged, especially in the D minor Quartet, to change many things since you were good enough to accept the dedication of the work; for it was my sacred duty to present to so great a master a work which conforms, if not in every respect, at least (forgive my lack of modesty) in many, to the demands which may be made on a work of art. How happy I should be if I knew it confirmed by your penetrating eye. I hope that it may.

And so I remain, with the expression of my profound respect for your genius, Your ever grateful

Antonín Dvořák.

Dvořák to Brahms in Vienna.—String Quartet in D minor, op. 34 (see 25).

36. BRAHMS TO DVOŘÁK IN REPLY

Dear Sir,

I should like to tell you only quite briefly that the rehearsals of your new works have won you the sympathy of the musicians here in quite an extraordinary measure.

So, for instance, yesterday at Hellmesberger's with the "Sextet" and the "Quartet". Hellmesberger is now extremely anxious to play through your two previous quartets, for this time his programmes are not, as formerly, laid down in advance.

If you can spare the score and parts, would you be kind enough to send them?

With best greetings,

Your entirely devoted

J. Brahms.

Brahms to Dvořák in Prague, X. 1879.—*Josef Hellmesberger*, sen. (1828-1893), teacher of violin at the Conservatoire in Vienna, leader of the Hofoper orchestra and leader of his own well-known Quartet.—For the Sextet and Quartet see nos. 26 and 33.

37. DVOŘÁK MAKES THE ACQUAINTANCE OF HANS RICHTER

Dear Friend,

...Only a few lines to tell you that I have just been to Vienna after receiving a telegram from Richter; I set out last Friday and was present at the performance of my III. Rhapsody, which was very well received and I had to show myself to the audience. I was sitting beside Brahms at the organ in the orchestra and Richter pulled me out. I *had* to come out. I must tell you that I won the sympathy of the whole orchestra at a stroke and that of all the novelties they tried over, and there were 60 as Richter told me, my Rhapsody was best liked. Richter *actually* embraced me on the spot and was very happy, as he said, to know me and promised that the Rhapsody would be repeated at an extraordinary concert in the Opera Theatre.

I promised to come to the performance of the Serenade and had to assure the Philharmonic that I would send them a symphony for the next season. The day after the concert, Richter gave a banquet at his house, in my honour so to speak, to which he invited all the Czech members of the orchestra. It was a grand evening which I shall not easily forget as long as I live. It was something like the one at Joachim's in summer.

The criticisms in the Vienna papers were good except for

one or two. I have kept the cuttings for you. Dr. Hanslick has not written yet but I went to see him and he said he liked it very much and was also at the general rehearsal with the score so that it must have interested him a good deal. He is going to write a longer article about me and so sent to Prague for some biographical data. And something more of interest. This III. Rhapsody is being played most of all: it has already been given in Berlin, Dresden, Budapest, Vienna, Carlsruhe, Münster, Wiesbaden etc. and will be performed in London very soon. I cannot write any more just now and so I close with friendly greetings and a hearty embrace.

Yours   Antonín Dvořák.

18 23/11 79.

I was also invited to visit the Director of the Hofoper, Jauner, who asked me to let him know about the performance of *Vanda*, that he was coming to Prague and would like to present it at the Hoftheater. Brahms recommended me to him very warmly. That would top everything if they were to perform my opera in Vienna! What?!

Dvořák to Alois Göbl at Sychrov (see 33).—*Hans Richter* (1843-1916), a distinguished German conductor, in the years 1875-1897, Kapellmeister of the Hofoper in Vienna and conductor of the Vienna Philharmonic, at the same time guest conductor at the Philharmonic Concerts in London and elsewhere. Dvořák's good friend and an especially ardent propagator of his works. He performed the III. Slavonic Rhapsody (see 35) with the Vienna Philharmonic on the 16th November 1879.—At Joachim's (see 33).— *F. Jauner* (1832-1900), at this time director of the Hofoper in Vienna. The opera "Vanda" was not performed in Vienna.

38. DVOŘÁK AND JOACHIM

Dear Mr. Dvořák,

I have just received by post your parcel with the Violin Concerto, and even though I shall not be able for some days to have the enjoyment of it for various performances and a journey to Frankfurt, still I must write now to thank you for the honour you have done me in dedicating it to me. My warm interest in your true musical blood, of which I have tried to give proof by the most careful and finished performance of that lovely work of genius, the Sextet in A, has enhanced for me the value of your dedication and of the feeling of professional friendship which dictated it. I shall now do what I can to strengthen it by showing the sincerity you desire and am looking forward to going through your work very soon and *con amore*.

In the meantime I remain,

Most respectfully and devotedly Yours,

Josef Joachim.

Joachim to Dvořák in Prague, 2. XII. 1879.—The celebrated *Violin Concerto in A minor*, op. 53, was written by Dvořák for Joachim to whom he also dedicated it. Joachim made some alterations in the solo part but himself never played it in public. Because of discussions dictated by consideration for Joachim's views, the revision of the Concerto dragged on from July 1879 till October 1882.

39. DVOŘÁK TO SIMROCK

Dear Mr. Simrock,

You ask me what I have written new. Well, not much, but still something.

I have so far two volumes of new *Waltzes* and *Eclogues* for piano (two hands). Should you be counting on these things, be good enough to let me know. Or would you rather wait till I come to Berlin? I expect the Waltzes to be quite a success.

With the Slavonic Dances we could perhaps wait till autumn. I feel now the need to write something serious. A Trio or a Violin Sonata—that would be what I shall need to keep me in good humour.

Becker writes me of the great successes achieved by the Quartet. He played it in Hannover, Halle, Hildesheim etc.

In Hamburg, too, where it was played by Bargheer, it was greatly appreciated. The criticisms were good.

    Au revoir very soon.

With greetings from

18 16/2 80.   Antonín Dvořák.

Simrock see 22.—The eight *Waltzes* for pianoforte solo, op. 54, were written
in December 1879 and in January 1880; the four *Eclogues* followed immediately and
were completed by the 7th February, 1880. Simrock published the Waltzes at once,
but the Eclogues first appeared in 1921 when they were published by the "Hudební
matice" in Prague.—The success of the first series of Slavonic Dances, op. 46, induced
Simrock to urge Dvořák to write a second series. He had, however, to wait for them till
1886 (see 96-97).—Dvořák did not then write a piano trio, but he did write a sonata—
the *Sonata for Violin and Piano in F major*, op. 57, composed between the 3rd and 17th
March 1880.—*Jean Becker* (1833-84), leader of the well-known Florentine Quartet,
at whose request Dvořák composed the "Slavonic" string quartet in E flat Major, op.
51.—*Karl Bargheer* (1831-1902), leader of the Philharmonic and professor at the Conservatoire in Hamburg.

40. DVOŘÁK AND LEOŠ JANÁČEK

Dear Friend,

    I had made preparations to go to Leipzig last week. Brahms
and Joachim were here, however, and besides a new presentation of Vanda was being given and so I was unable to get
away. I think, however, that I shall come on Saturday or Sunday
for sure.

    I should like to hear a Gewandhaus concert. Next Thursday
will probably be the last concert, is it not? Please meet me at the
station. I shall come either on Saturday evening or on Sunday
forenoon. If I stop in Dresden, I shall wire you.

    Au revoir,

Yours

                                                     Dvořák.

Dvořák in Prague to Leoš Janáček in Leipzig, 19. II. 1880. Leoš Janáček (see 14),
who was studying at the Conservatoire in Leipzig in the year 1879-80, informed Dvořák
that Karl Reinecke was going to give two Slavonic Dances at the Gewandhaus concert
on the 23rd February 1880. — Brahms and Joachim gave a concert in Prague on the
11th February 1880. — The opera "Vanda" was performed by the Czech Theatre under
new direction on the 13th of the same month.

41. AT JOACHIM'S IN BERLIN

18 1/4 80.

Dear Friend,

I must tell you that I arrived in Berlin safely and experienced many happy moments. Yesterday I played the Sonata (among other things) with Joachim and he was very delighted with it. Today the quartet is playing and I am greatly looking forward to it. Tomorrow we shall go through the Concerto really properly.

Scarcely had I returned—and there were these "danged" proofs waiting for me.

My warm greetings to you and all the other gentlemen.

Yours

Ant. Dvořák.

Dvořák from Berlin to Göbl at Sychrov.—The Sonata for Violin and Piano in F major, see 39.—The reference is to the Violin Concerto, see 38.

42. DVOŘÁK VISITS EHLERT IN WIESBADEN

7 a. m. in Wiesbaden,
18 18/8 80.

Dear Friend,

I have been here in Wiesbaden two days already and like it very much. I happened to meet Řebíček near the Theatre so that I did not need to look for him long, for which I was glad. Ehlert, whom I really came here to see, was not at home: we had to take a carriage to Falkenstein where he is spending the summer with his wife (a very charming lady) because of her poor health. On Thursday we were invited to his house for dinner. When I (D. V.) come to see you again I shall have a great deal to tell you, and I am looking forward to it.

Yours

Dvořák.

. At the moment I am sailing down the Rhine to Cologne.

Dvořák to Göbl at Sychrov.—Dvořák went to Wiesbaden to visit L. Ehlert (see 30).—Řebíček see 34.

43. DVOŘÁK TO RICHTER

18 28/9 80.

Dear Sir,

I am pleased to be able to inform you that I have just finished the new symphony, all that remains to be done is the instrumentation and the copying out of the parts with which I hope to be finished by the end of the month. You could, therefore, count on having it by the second or third concert for certain, in which case I would ask you once more to recommend my new work to your colleagues, for which please accept now my warmest thanks.

With kindest regard and warm greetings,

Your ever grateful

Ant. Dvořák.

Hans Richter see 37.—In the first half of October 1880, Dvořák wrote the *Symphony in D major* for the Vienna Philharmonic and dedicated it to Richter. It was actually Dvořák's *sixth* symphony, but Simrock published it in 1881 as the *first*.

44. CZECH EDITION OF THE GIPSY MELODIES

Dear Mr Simrock,

I wish to tell you quite briefly that I have just completed the working out and instrumentation of the new Symphony.

Next week I shall probably be going to Vienna where the Philharmonic will try it over. I have made every effort to produce a living work which would also give me pleasure.

Now I am going to work at piano duets under the title: *Legends*, and hope to be finished with them next month. In addition I have several new things for piano which I wish to give you.

And now I have a request. From what I hear, the Gipsy Melodies are in lively demand here in Bohemia but with Czech text. Would it not be possible to publish the vocal parts separately with Czech text, or if you were to publish the whole cycle with Czech text you would certainly not stand to lose anything by it, and you would give me great pleasure, as it is an attention I am due my countrymen to make it possible for them to sing my songs in the Czech language.

Please write me what you think about it.

With kindest regards,

Your ever devoted

Ant. Dvořák.

The new symphony is that in D major (see 43).—The *"Legends"* for piano (four hands), op. 59, were written between February 12th and March 22 1881.—The songs entitled *"Gipsy Melodies"*, op. 55, to words by the Czech poet *Adolf Heyduk* (1835-1923), composed between January 18th and February 23rd 1880, were published by Simrock at first with German text only. He granted Dvořák's request, however, and in February 1881 the songs came out with Czech text and an English translation (by Natalie Macfarren).

45. RICHTER AND THE D MAJOR SYMPHONY

Vienna, 18 23/11 80.

Dear Friend,

I am in Vienna where I have heard so many lovely things that I can't even begin to write about them. Richter likes the

Symphony immensely and embraced me after each movement, and the first performance will be on the 26th.

Then I am off to London. I am returning to Prague, today. When are you coming, I can hardly wait to see you.

Yours

Dvořák.

Dvořák to Göbl at Sychrov.—Dvořák went to Vienna to play over the D major symphony to Richter on the piano. Richter did not, however, perform the composition till the 15th May, 1882, at a concert of the Philharmonic Society in London (see 53 and 54). For postponement of the Vienna performance see 46 and 47.

46. VIENNA PERFORMANCE POSTPONED

My dear Friend,

Forgive me for being so long in letting you hear from me. Our orchestra has been so overburdened with work lately that I have put off your lovely composition to the 6th Concert (the beginning of March), when we shall have enough time to prepare your Symphony in a way worthy of it. I have already included it in my London programme. If you can, entrust me with the *first* performance of this magnificent work. In any case, the months of January and February are, with their carnival entertainments, not suitable for serious works, and the few weeks will pass very quickly.

With kindest regards and Best Wishes for the New Year, I remain, Your sincerely devoted friend,

Hans Richter.

Richter to Dvořák, XII. 1880.—At the concert of the Vienna Philharmonic held on 26. XII. 1880, the programme consisted of: the first performance of Brahms's Tragic Overture, then Prelude and Liebestod from Wagner's Tristan, arias from Haendel's Oratoria "Semele" and Beethoven's Eighth. (See also 47.)

47. DVOŘÁK REPLIES TO RICHTER

My dear Hofkapellmeister,   Prague, 18 1/1 81

Nothing could have given me a pleasanter surprise on New
Year's Day than the receipt of your lines from which I learn
that you wish to perform my work at the 6th Concert. I should
in any case have found it almost impossible to come at Christmas, which every father of a family likes to spend in the circle
of his dear ones, and then my time was very much taken up with
the first performance of my "Stabat Mater", when I had to be
present at rehearsals. As I said before, I shall be very grateful
to the gentlemen for performing the symphony, even though at
a later date, and emphasize, once more, that I attach the greatest
importance to the *first* performance being in Vienna under *your*
incomparable direction.
    Till then I remain,
                    Your ever devoted
                                        Ant. Dvořák.

Evidently in consequence of a lack of good-will on the part of the responsible
functionaries of the Vienna Philharmonic, Dvořák's D major Symphony was not performed in Vienna after all.

48. A NEW OPERA

...As regards "Dimitri", Father wished me to take it from
Šebor and to give it to someone else, both he and Maýr thought
to Dvořák. Jeřábek, in the meantime, had read my libretto and
I asked him to return it to me and then Maýr gave it to Dvořák
to read... Maýr then came with the news that Dvořák liked it
very much and had asked Maýr if he could speak with the gen-
tleman-librettist. Maýr, who had not at first divulged whom the
libretto was by, replied that the librettist wore skirts: where-

upon it was arranged that Dvořák should come to see us on the forenoon of January 6th—Epiphany... Dvořák arrived on the appointed day and Father had a long talk with him. Dvořák once more asked to have the libretto and then came to see me a number of times to discuss various things etc. Dvořák showed it to some of his friends... Now I must make the changes for Dvořák and I am somehow out of humour with it—unpleasant work...

From the Diary of Marie Červinková-Riegerová, January 1881.—Marie Červin-ková (1854-1895), daughter of the eminent Czech political leader, Dr. František L. Rieger, was the author of the libretti of Dvořák's operas "Dimitri" and "The Jacobin". The Libretto of "Dimitri", whose plot is a continuation of that of Mussorgski's opera "Boris Godunov", and is taken from the same historic period of anarchy which followed Boris's death during the reign of the Pretender, the false Dimitri, was originally written for Dvořák's friend, *Karel Šebor* (1843-1903), but when the latter had long deferred the work of musical composition, the author offered it to Dvořák. His "Dimitri" was composed in the years 1881-2 (completed on the 16th August 1882).

49. DR RIEGER ON DVOŘÁK

...Dvořák is a musician through and through and creates, like all real talents, almost unconsciously. I am glad that he has taken to your libretto. Everything one can learn has always had much smaller value for me than what we have from our mothers. I am looking forward to your "Demetrius", with Dvořák's music, making its way out into the world very soon...

Dr. František L. Rieger to his daughter, Marie Červinková, 3. V. 1881.—See 48.

50. DVOŘÁK'S PERSONAL APPEARANCE

The figure of Antonín Dvořák was a somewhat unusual one. He used to come to our musical meetings at Urbánek's shop quite often, but irregularly, and both Urbáneks showed him the honour due to his importance. Even then (c. 1881), he was Smetana's acknowledged successor and a very fertile composer on the way to world fame.

Dvořák was interesting as a person—he was at that time about 40. Not very tall, rather thick-set, but restless, unable to stand still a minute. His face not over-refined, but so distinctive that you could not but remember it. Dark-complexioned, with a short, tousled beard which sometimes stood on end; features rather sullen with two vertical furrows above his nose. His brown eyes kept wandering abstractedly and had a far-away expression. Later Dvořák wore a pince-nez for reading but perched it almost on the end of his nose beside a wart. He rarely took off his outside coat even in winter and kept his hat—a bowler, on his head. Only occasionally, when engaged in conversation about musical matters, would he take it off mechanically and put it down somewhere, but in a little while he put it on his head again.

From the Memoirs of L. K. Žižka (1864-) a Prague bookseller and writer who, in the years 1881-91, was shop-assistant in Fr. A. Urbánek's music-shop beside the Czech National Theatre, where the musical fraternity, including Dvořák, used to meet for a chat and to look through the musical novelties. The extract is from the book "Masters Great and Small, Recollections of Czech Musicians".—Both Urbáneks: the leading Czech music publisher, *František A. Urbánek* (1842-1919) and his brother *Velebín Urbánek* (1853-1892) his partner, editor of the music magazine "Dalibor" and later agent for some of Dvořák's concerts.

51. FURTHER SUCCESSES

18 3/10 81.

Dear Friend,

This is just to tell you of the great success of "The Pig-headed Ones". Further details later. Hanslík has spoken and in great style. I am keeping that number of the *Presse* for you. He laid it on thick and no mistake. In Vienna a lot of things are in preparation this year: the II. Rhapsody, the Symphony (D major), and for Hellmesberger I am writing a new quartet at his request.

Your affectionate

Dvořák.

Dvořák to A. Göbl at Sychrov.—The comic one-act opera "The Pig-headed Ones", on a text by Adolf Štolba, was composed in autumn 1874 and was first performed at the Czech Interim Theatre in Prague on the 2nd October 1881. The pig-headed ones in the opera are a boy and girl who, in spite, or because of, their parents' encouragement refuse to acknowledge that they are in love with each other and do so only under the pressure of jealousy awakened in them by the cunning trick of an old gossip.—Bendl see 16.—Dr Ed. Hanslick (see 18) published in the Neue Freie Presse an enthusiastic notice of Dvořák's "Legends".—For Hellmesberger (see 36), Dvořák wrote the String Quartet in C major between the 25th October and the 10th November 1881.

52. JOACHIM AND SIMROCK VISITED AGAIN

Dear Friend, Berlin, 18 19/10 81.

I am here in Berlin again. I cannot omit to write you a few lines from here, too, for you are everywhere in my thoughts and I am looking forward to visiting you on the return journey... This morning I was at Joachim's and arrived very opportunely. They were playing the Mendelssohn and Brahms Quartets for their next performance. He promised to play my D minor Quartet this year. Joachim liked the "Legends" immensely and in Vienna they are also popular. Simrock told me that Brahms played them with Prof. Door. It seems I have made a good hit— and Simrock certainly has not come off badly. On Friday I shall meet Joachim in Dresden where he is giving a concert and on Saturday we shall arrive with the afternoon train at Sychrov and back to Prague on Sunday.

With affectionate greetings Your

Dvořák.

Dvořák to A. Göbl at Sychrov.—For Joachim see 33.—The D minor Quartet see 25.—*Anton Door* (1833-1919), teacher of piano at the Conservatoire of the Society of Friends of Music in Vienna.

63

53. RICHTER HONOURED BY DEDICATION

My dear and noble Friend,

On my return from London I find your splendid work awaiting me whose dedication makes me truly proud. Words do not suffice to express my thanks: a performance worthy of this noble work must prove to you how highly I value it and the honour of the dedication.

Forgive me for not having written immediately after my arrival in Vienna (Jan. 4th). The preparations for the Philharmonic Concerts and theatre work of all kinds did not allow of my studying the Symphony properly and without a *thorough* acquaintance with it, I did not wish to write to you. If I do not manage to give a performance of your Symphony in this series of Philharmonic Concerts, I shall give a special concert of my own in order to present your work to the public before the end of the season. It will certainly be performed at the 2nd concert of my London season as well as one of your Rhapsodies; I gave the one in A flat last year.

Once more my warmest thanks and kindest regards,

Your ever devoted,

Hans Richter.

The letter is dated from Vienna, 26. I. 1882.—For the performance of the D major Symphony see 46.

54. LONDON SUCCESS OF THE NEW SYMPHONY

London, May 13th 1882.

My dear Friend,

This morning the first rehearsal of your *magnificent* work. I am proud of the dedication. The orchestra is enthusiastic. Monday the 15th is the première. At 8 p. m. Am sure of a great

5. The Interim Theatre in Prague where Dvořák was employed as a member of the orchestra in 1862–1871.

6. Johannes Brahms.

success. It is also studied and rehearsed with love. More after the performance.

With warmest greetings,

Your

Hans Richter.

Hans Richter in London to Dvořák in Prague, 13. V. 1882.

55. DVOŘÁK TO SIMROCK

Dear Fritz, Prague 16. 9. 82.

So you are back in Berlin. I was there, too, and played through the Violin Concerto with Joachim twice—he is very delighted with it. I am very glad that it will be done with at last! The revised work lay a whole two years with Joachim. He was himself kind enough to make the alterations in the solo part. I must still only change something in the Finale and make the instrumentation more delicate in a number of places. I must go to Berlin again at the beginning of November, by when I hope everything will be finished, and Joachim will have a rehearsal with orchestra at the Hochschule.

And now something else—on September 28th, my Dimitri will be given! Will you be present at it? I wrote to Hanslick yesterday. He is perhaps coming with Brahms. Jauner wrote me that Pollini asks to have the score of *The Peasant a Rogue* at once. Have you let him have word about it? Don't put off—it is urgent. I am very much looking forward to the score. Joachim is playing the C major Quartet. Otherwise nothing important!

I have still a gigantic amount of work—I must rehearse, too—the Overture is not finished yet. Of that later!

With kind regards—and give 1000 marks apiece to

Your

Tonda.

Hearty greetings to all.

Violin Concerto see 38.—The opera "Dimitri" (see 48) was first performed by the New Czech Theatre in Prague on the 8th Oct. 1882. Jauner viz 37.—*Bernhard Pollini* (or Baruch Pohl, 1838-1897), director of the Municipal Theatre in Hamburg, where he produced Dvořák's opera "The Peasant a Rogue" (see 28) on the 3rd January 1883.— 1000 marks apiece: refers evidently to the fee for the String Quartet in C major, op. 61 and to the Overture to the popular play "Josef Kajetán Tyl", published by Simrock under the title "Mein Heim". (*J. K. Tyl*, the first Czech playwright of note and the author of the first part of the present-day Czechoslovak National Anthem).

56. DVOŘÁK TO SIMROCK ON THE SUCCESS OF HIS OPERAS

Prague, 16. 10. 82.

Dear Friend,

A thousand pities that you weren't in Dresden: you would certainly have rejoiced heartily at the splendid success and the exemplary presentation. Schuch did a really excellent bit of work. Everything went off without a hitch and the nuances in the orchestra and chorus were wonderful. Mr. Bulss and Madam Schuch as well as Mr. Decarli (Martin), Erl (Jeník) and Madam Jensen were excellent. The Overture was immediately followed by a strom of applause as were almost all the arias. Especially, however, the Prince's aria was so beautifully performed that the audience demanded an encore. In short, everything was splendid and the audience very animated. I was called for after each act. Schuch is very anxious for you to come to the next performance. I should go there again, too. Perhaps I shall be in Berlin next week and that would be the best opportunity. Yesterday at the 7th performance of Dimitri, Mr. Rosa, director of the English opera was here from London. Pollini wanted to come as well. Do let me hear from you.

With kindest regards, Dvořák.

The Hofoper in Dresden performed the opera "The Peasant a Rogue" on the 24th October 1882 under the direction of the chef d'opera *Ernst Schuch* (1847-1914). The celebrated baritone, *Paul Bulls* (1847-1902) sang the part of the Prince, Madam Clementine Schuch, née Procházková—Betuška.—*Carlo Rosa*, (Karl Rose) at that time an opera producer in London and New York.

57. DVOŘÁK TO HIS PARENTS

Dear Father and Mother,

I am enclosing 20 gulden for the rent along with a small contribution, that is, 15 gulden, and five gulden for some "extras".

I was in Dresden some days ago where they were giving a performance of "The Peasant a Rogue", with what success you have probably read in the papers.

In short, they liked my opera very much and the audience called for me very stormily. The Queen of Saxony was also at the theatre, which is undoubtedly a great honour.

Next winter they will give "Dimitri" also in Dresden and in London. The Peasant then in Hamburg and Leipzig.

On December 6th I am going to Budapest to conduct the new Symphony. I am looking forward very much to getting to know Budapest.

This week still I am going to Berlin and Dresden.

In the meantime God keep you all and prosper you,

Your grateful son,

Antonín.

Prague, 18 1/11 82,
on All Saints' Day.

Dvořák's father František (see 1) and his wife Anna lived, at this time, in Kladno to which they had moved about the middle of 1860. Dvořák's mother died on the 14th December 1882.—The opera "Dimitri" was not performed either in Germany or in England; "The Peasant a Rogue" was given not only in Dresden but also in Hamburg (see 55) and in Vienna (see 76).—Dvořák did not go to Budapest as he intended.

58. LONDON SUCCESS OF THE II. RHAPSODY

Dear Friend,   Prague, 18 17/7 83.

I certainly do not trouble you too much with letters but all the same I am not lazy. At my concert yesterday—June 11th— your second Slavonic Rhapsody met with storms of applause

67

from the London audience. The valiant orchestra—at first a little stultified—soon found delight in your lovely work; and after the musicians had become familiar with the melodies and the abundance of rhythmical life, they performed the Rhapsody with enthusiastic fire and élan.

Best Greetings,

Your devoted

Hans Richter

Richter in London to Dvořák in Prague, 12. VI. 1883.

59. FURTHER COMPOSITIONS AND SUCCESSES

My dear good Friend, Prague, 18 17/7 83.

...Often, very often, I think of you and imagine how, if I had you here—or you me there—we should talk of different things—and there would be plenty for us to say... Perhaps you would be interested if I sent you the Silhouettes which have just come out for 4 hands. They are excellently arranged by Th. Kirchner of Dresden, are agreeable to play and sound very well. I shall forward them today and, along with them, the solo part of the Piano Concerto which has also just come out. On my next visit you will play me something from it.

It appears that the piano concerto will awaken quite a lot of interest in the world, at least I got word lately from Ehlert and Brahms that both are very anxious to become acquainted with the work. Needless to say Hainauer forwarded it to them immediately. From London, too, I got a recommendation to a pianist there, Beringer, who will play my concerto in London during the coming season and who is to visit me in the first half of August. Richter wrote, too, that my II. Rhapsody was a great success. At first the musicians, so he says, found it a little strange,

68

it was new for them, but at the second and third rehearsals they got to like it better and better, and at the concert then they played like devils. The Overture to "Tyl" in the Crystal Palace also got a great reception, at least from what I read in a German paper.

From Frankfurt, the director of the Museum Concerts, Müller, also wrote that the Symphony and Sextet were very much appreciated and enclosed 45 marks (as *Ehrenhonorar*). I must show you the letter. So you see that the people like me a little after all and think something of me and have *understanding*, too. If it was only like that here with us. The rest will keep till I see you (D. V.) at Sychrov.

Your affectionate friend

Dvořák.

Dvořák to Göbl at Sychrov.—*The Silhouettes*, a cycle of 12 compositions for piano, op. 8, 1879, composed on themes from his first two symphonies (C minor and B flat major) and from the songs "The Cypresses" (all in 1865). Published by Fr. Hoffmeister in Leipzig in 1880 in the original version and in an arrangement as piano duets by Theodor Kirchner.—*The Piano Concerto in G minor*, op. 33, 1876, was published in 1883 by Hainauer in Vratislav (now Wroclaw)—The German pianist *Oskar Beringer* (1844-1922), resident in London, played this Concerto a number of times. Dvořák, on his first visit to London in March 1884 (see 66), was his guest.—For Richter's performance of the Slavonic Rhapsody in London see 58.—Prof. *Karl Müller* (1818-1894), conductor of the Cecilian Musical Society in Frankfurt-on-Main.

60. LEOŠ JANÁČEK ON DVOŘÁK

...Of Janáček's friendship with Dvořák, his elder by 13 years, Janáček told me that they used to go for long excursions together on which they were generally silent. Dvořák spoke very little. Often he gave no reply to questions. Janáček opposed very strongly the opinion often expressed as to Dvořák not being intelligent. On the contrary, he maintained, Dvořák was continually deep in thought. "His intelligence was of quite a special

order," says Janáček. "He thought exclusively in tone and paid
no heed to anything else..."

Max Brod: From the book "Leoš Janáček–Life and Work".–*Dr. Max Brod*
(b. 1884), a Prague German author, journalist and critic, an enthusiastic admirer and
propagator of the works of the Moravian composer, Leoš Janáček. He wrote a number
of studies on him and translated the libretto of his operas into German.

61. DVOŘÁK'S PLANS

He wishes now to write pieces for piano duets–something
characteristic from the Böhmerwald (Šumava), Simrock, he
says, wants it: but I don't feel too keen about it, said Dvořák,–
I haven't any proper titles. Schumann exhausted all the suitable
titles and anyhow all that kind of thing has been done before
and it is difficult to find new and characteristic and original
titles for the different pieces for piano: Said I: What does it
matter about titles if there is only the music? Oh, there's no
question about the music, replied Dvořák. I've got that; but
I have no titles. Then he asked me if I couldn't give him some
suitable poetic titles–like pictures–and always add a few words
of description, that he would then get the spirit of it and fill in
the rest. He only wanted, as I saw, to have some kind of motif,
some impulse to set him thinking...

From the Diary of Marie Červinková (see 48), September 1883 (see 49). The cycle of
piano duets "*From the Bohemian Forest*", op. 68, was undoubtedly written under the influence of the impresisons from the wanderings with Janáček through the south of Bohemia, between September 1883 and January 12th 1884. Published by Simrock in 1884.

62. VISIT TO BRAHMS

...I was in Vienna some days ago where I spent some lovely
days with Dr. Brahms who had just come back from Wiesbaden.
I have never seen him in such a happy mood. We were together

every noon and evening, and had much to talk about. He seems to take pleasure in my company and I am so captivated by his kindness both as an artist and as a man that I can find it in my heart to love him. What a heart and mind the man has! You know how reserved he is as regards his creative work even towards his dearest friends, but he has never been so with me. My wish to hear something from his new Symphony he granted at once and played the first and last movements. I say, and I am not exaggerating, that this work surpasses both his earlier Symphonies, if not perhaps in greatness and monumentality of expression, then certainly—in beauty! In it there is a mood which you will not find so often in Brahms. What lovely melodies are there! It is pure love, and on hearing it your heart melts within you! Remember what I say and when you hear the Symphony you will say that I heard aright. But enough. The work will be an adornment to art and I congratulate you in advance.

Your

A. D.

On Sunday the 14th, Ondříček is playing my Violin Concerto.

Dvořák to Simrock in Berlin, 10.X. 1883.—The Symphony referred to is Brahms's Third Symphony in F major, op. 90.—Dvořák's Violin Concerto (see 38) was played for the first time by the famous Czech violinist, František Ondříček (1857–1922), all his life one of Dvořák's most enthusiastic admirers. The first performance took place in Prague on 14. X. 1883.

63. ONDŘÍČEK AND DVOŘÁK'S CONCERTO

Dear Friend,   Vienna, Nov. 15th 1883.

I spoke here to Sarasate and although he knows that I am going to play your Concerto here, he spoke of the work in a very equivocal way, which made me so angry that I told him that

71

he did not know the work. Whereupon he remarked that he had played it from sight, which I do not believe, because such a violinist has yet to be born. Still worse was what he said about your Concerto to Kopta in Graz: he said that Joachim will certainly not play it, that it is nothing but *teeteetee* and old-fashioned form. Chiefly for this reason I have not called on him again and have not given him my photograph which he asked me for.

I wanted to play your Concerto in Hamburg on the 23rd of this month, but they turned it down—why I do not know but shall find out. In spite of that I have put the work on my programme both for Frankfurt and Bremen. I shall also play it here at my big concert for the second time, of course with orchestra, in the large Musikvereinsaal.

So you see, my dear Friend, I give you no cause for complaint and should be glad if I could play your Concerto in London in Spring.

With kind regards to your wife and yourself,

I am, Your devoted friend,

Fr. Ondříček.

Sarasate played Beethoven *a l'espagnole*—something frightful, small wonder he cannot understand your Concerto.

See 62.—Ondříček gave a first performance of Dvořák's Concerto in Vienna on the 2nd December 1883, at a concert of the Vienna Philharmonic under the baton of Hans Richter.—*Pablo Sarasate* (1844-1908), the celebrated Spanish violin virtuoso and one-time professor at the Conservatoires in Philadelphia, Graz and Munich.

64. PREPARATIONS FOR A FIRST VISIT TO ENGLAND

Dear Sir,

I sent you word three days ago that I shall arrive in London on Saturday, March 8th and shall be met by Mr. Berger. Thank you for your kind invitation which I have pleasure in accepting and am looking forward to spending a pleasant evening in your company.

I shall bring with me the Hymnus which has already been translated into *German*. I shall also be able to give you more information about it.

For the present I beg you to accept my respectful greetings,

Yours sincerely,

A. Dvořák.

Dvořák to Henry Littleton in London, March 1884, written in English.—Henry Littleton, proprietor of the publishing firm of Novello, Ewer and Co., London.—In March 1884, Dvořák made the first of a series of nine visits to English towns, each of which was a splendid success for him both as composer and conductor.—Beringer see 59.—Hymnus, "The Heirs of the White Mountain" (see 16) was published by the firm of Novello in 1885. For its first performance under Dvořák's baton see also 83.

65. THE "HUSSITE" OVERTURE

Dear Friend,   Prague, 18 5/3 84.

...I cannot give you my score for comparison till I come back from London. I am leaving for there this evening as I have been informed by the Concert Committee that a change has been made: instead of at the beginning of May, I am to conduct in London on the 13th and 19th of March. A letter has just come from London. I am to conduct at the Crystal Palace. I shall be back about the 23rd of March.

With warm greetings,

Dvořák.

From Dvořák to Simrock in Berlin. The letter evidently refers to the *"Hussite" dramatic overture,* op. 67, which Dvořák composed between the 9th August and the 9th September 1883 for the festive inauguration of the Czech National Theatre in Prague which took place on the 18th November 1883. The Overture, which has as its content the ethic significance of the glorious epoch of the Hussite Rising in the history of the Czech nation (the beg. of the 15th cent.) as a struggle for the great idea of national freedom, is based, in addition to several original themes, on two motifs from old Czech chorales: the St. Václav (Wenceslaus) Hymn from the 13th century and the Hussite chorale: "Ye who are God's warriors" from the 15th century.

66. IN ENGLAND FOR THE FIRST TIME

...To complete my report, I must tell you that we arrived in London on March 8th at 6 p. m. The only places we broke our journey at were Cologne and Brussels. The crossing was marvellous, the sea absolutely calm and we set foot on English soil perfectly fit. The next day we saw the name Dvořák in almost all the papers, some having had the "ř" and the "á" specially cast, while others wrote "Dvorak". Dvořák is staying with the pianist Beringer and I with a countryman, Mr. Zavrtal, 9 English miles away...

Extract from a letter by Jindřich Kàan to Velebín Urbánek (see 50).—Dvořák's first visit was to London where he stayed from March 8th to 27th 1884 (see letters following). Dvořák, who learned English relatively quickly, was accompanied this time by *Jindřich Kàan* (1858-1926), composer and professor of piano at the Prague Conservatoire.—Beringer see 59.—*Ladislav Josef Zavertal* (1849-1886) born in Milan as the son of a Czech father, lived in London at that time as bandmaster of His Majesty's Forces. He got to know Dvořák in 1880 when visiting Prague for the performance of his opera "Night in Florence".

67. DVOŘÁK'S FIRST LONDON SUCCESS

...On Monday there was the first rehearsal with the choir in the Albert Hall, an immense building which can comfortably seat 12,000 people. When I appeared at the desk, I was welcomed with such a thunder of applause that it took some considerable time before there was quiet again. I was so deeply touched with the warmth of the ovation that I could not speak a word, and, in any case, it would not have been of any use as nobody would have understood me. ...The director of the Society, which performs only oratorios, *Mr. Barnby*, who conducted my "Stabat Mater" last year, had this time prepared and studied everything so thoroughly that the rehearsal went off very well indeed. The next day there was a rehearsal with the orchestra and, in the afternoon, with the soloists. They are the foremost artists in London and especially the tenor and the contralto are lovely voices. I must, however, give you an idea of the size of the orchestra and choir. Don't get a shock! 250 sopranos, 160 contraltos, 180 tenors and 250 basses; the orchestra: 24 first violins, 20 second violins, 16 violas, 16 cellos and 16 double-basses.

The effect of such an immense corpus was truly magnificent. It is, indeed, indescribable.

On Tuesday Littleton gave a dinner in my honour. About 150 persons were invited, among them the leading artists and critics. Each one welcomed me most heartily and gave me a warm hand-shake. That evening was devoted exclusively to my compositions... We stayed till half-past two in the morning.

Littleton is a very charming man and fabulously rich; it is really wonderful the appointments and the whole style of living at his princely house. At his request I shall write a new oratorio for the celebrations in Leeds...

...At the concert my appearance was greeted with a storm of applause. The general enthusiasm grew from item to item, and, at the end, the applause was so great that I had to thank the audience again and again. At the same time the orchestra and choir overwhelmed me from the other side with the heartiest ovations. In short it turned out better than I could ever have hoped for.

All this has led me to the conclusion that here in England a happier time, God grant it may be so, has begun for me which, I hope, *will bear Czech art in general good fruit.* The English are a good, warm-hearted and music-loving nation and it is well known that when once they take a liking to someone, they remain faithful to him. God grant it may be so with me...

Dvořák in London to Velebín Urbánek (see 50) in Prague.—At his first public appearance in London, Dvořák conducted his sacred cantata "Stabat Mater" at the Albert Hall. The rehearsal of which he speaks in the letter took place on March 10th, the concert itself on the 13th March 1884. The solo parts were sung by A. Williams (soprano), Patey (contralto), Fred King (tenor) and Charles Lloyd (bass). The work was rehearsed by Sir *Joseph Barnby* (1838-1896), founder and conductor of the oratorio concerts at the Albert Hall, who had presented Stabat Mater on March 10th of the previous year (1883).—Henry Littleton see 64.—The new oratorio for Leeds: "Saint Ludmilla" see also 101.

68. LONDON IMPRESSIONS (I)

Dear Friend,

I beg you not to be vexed with me for not having sent you any news, but I am so taken up the whole day with rehearsals, visiting and other things that I am glad when I come home in the afternoon to throw myself down on the sofa and rest a little.

I only wish you could see for yourself this city, its bustle and life—it would simply take your breath away. All attempts at description are vain; anyone who has not seen and heard it would not believe it.

Imagine only this: Kàan is staying with Zavertal, 9 English miles from here, that is as far as from Prague to Kralupy or to Říčany, or again to Dobřichovice and then to somewhere near Český Brod. Imagine this huge area a mass of houses and streets with a network of railways and you have some small idea what London is like. Or: imagine the New Town Theatre about five times as big and you will know what the Albert Hall is like where 10,000 people listened to Stabat Mater and 1050 musicians and singers played and sang—and then the enormous organ. Imagine then the most wonderful co-ordination of the whole ensemble and you will be able to imagine the impression of this or that composition.

When they sing Händel's Messiah here and they come to the jubilant Hallelujahs, then the whole audience rises to their feet, waving their hats and handkerchiefs. I am giving you only a short account of all this so that you can have some slight idea what Kàan and I have experienced here.

With greetings to yourself and all the others,

I remain, Your Friend

A. Dvořák.

Dvořák to Karel Bendl (see 16) in Prague, March 1884.—Kàan and Zavertal see 66.—The wooden building of the New Town Theatre with a circular ground plan stood from 1859-1885 on the site of the present-day National Museum in Prague. Performances were given there in summer.

69. LONDON IMPRESSIONS (II)

Manchestr Square W.
12, Hinde Street.   London, Friday 21st March 1884.

Dear Father,

I got your letter and was very glad that you, too, remembered me. Who could have thought that far across the sea, in this enormous London, I should one day celebrate triumphs such as few foreign artists have known! I shan't make any long story about it, perhaps you have all read in Kladno what the newspapers wrote about my great successes.

Just to give you a slight idea of what this London looks like and how terribly big it is, I shall tell you the following:

If all the *Czech inhabitants of the whole of Bohemia* were put together, they would not number as many as the inhabitants of London. And if all the inhabitants of the town of Kladno were to visit that enormous hall where I conducted my Stabat Mater, there would still be plenty of room—for that is how huge the *Albert Hall is!*

Yesterday I had my second concert in St. James's Hall where I again achieved the most splendid success! I cannot tell you how great is the honour and respect the English people here show me. Everywhere they write and talk about me and say that I am the *lion* of this year's musical season in London! Two banquets have already been given here in my honour, and on Monday, a third, and a very grand one, is being given by the society of artists, the "Philharmonia", which invited me to London. In September I shall have to come here again, but still farther to beyond London. It is the big industrial town of *Worchester*, where I shall again conduct Stabat Mater. For next year and '86 I already have offers to come to England and shall have to write new compositions.

From this you can judge how they like me and value me. In some of the papers there was also mention made of you, that

77

I come of poor parents and that my father was a butcher and innkeeper in Nelahozeves and did everything to give his son a proper educatian, *Honour be to you for that!* When I get back to Prague I shall visit you at Kladno. Till then God keep you.

With a loving embrace,

Your grateful son,

Antonín.

Dvořák in London to his father František (see 1 and 57), in Kladno, Bohemia. —Dvořák's second concert took place at the smaller *St. James's Hall* on March 20th 1884 with the London Philharmonic Society. Dvořák conducted his "Hussite" overture, the D major Symphony, op. 60, the II. Slavonic Rhapsody and the "Gipsy Melodies" sung by the tenor Winch.—The dinner given by the Philharmonic Society was at the Café Royal on Monday the 24th March.—For Dvořák's second visit to England (to Worcester) see also 79 and 80.

70. DVOŘÁK TO SIMROCK IN BERLIN

Prague 18 1/4 84.

Dear Friend,

I came back from London two days ago where I had the most tremendous success. I should have liked to send you a fuller report from London but my time was so taken up with rehearsals, invitations etc. that I was glad to make use of the remaining time to rest. I cannot describe to you in words the overpowering impression of the Stabat. It was breath-taking. A choir (excellent) of 1000 voices and an orchestra 160 strong! Indescribable! I am awaiting the proofs. More another time.

With best greetings,

Your

Antonín Dvořák.

71. DVOŘÁK AS CONDUCTOR (I)

Dvořák is not one of those "salon" conductors whose concern is that their pose at the desk should make an impression and that the baton in their hands may describe elegant lines; he conducts modestly, with those involuntary movements of the body which show that the spirit, in the process of reproduction, is living over once more the composition it created; yet he conducts with that concentrated musical devotion which fires the masses and communicates itself to each of the performing musicians, fills him with enthusiasm for his task and makes of each one an indispensible part of the whole. If Dvořák had not become a famous composer, he could have become a celebrated conductor—his musical talent is universal and as aesthetically typical in composition as it is in the conducting of musical works.

Emanuel Chvála (1851-1924), leading Czech musical critic, for many years musical critic of the Czech dailies—Národní Politika and Politika and a composer. In Czech musical circles, his word as a critic carried great weight.—The extract is from a notice dating from 1896.

72. DVOŘÁK AS CONDUCTOR (II)

I saw Dvořák as a conductor at one of the Popular Concerts. But surprisingly enough not a trace of nervousness and his gestures were directed entirely towards the score. It seemed to me that at the desk he had grown taller, but it was perhaps only an illusion born of the excitement of the moment.

From the book by L. K. Žižka (see 50).

73. DVOŘÁK AS CONDUCTOR (III)

Do you remember Dvořák when he had finished conducting and turned to face the audience? The proud forehead with its almost hard expression, with its deep furrows and with that lovely spiritualized eye? That is always how I picture him when I call him to mind. So composed, so contemptuous of the daily bustle and tumult...

Ladislav Dolanský (1857-1910), Czech musical critic and writer, did important research work on Smetana.—Extract from his book "Musical Memoirs".

74. DVOŘÁK REPLIES TO ONDŘÍČEK

Dear Friend,   Prague, 18 9/4 84.

I was in Plzeň for a few days and conducted Stabat Mater and so it was not possible for me to reply to your letter till today. First of all thank you for your congratulations on my London successes which were truly splendid, only a pity that you could not be present. Joachim could not play my Concerto (though he was willing) because the Philharmonic would not consent to my conducting at other concerts before conducting with them, seeing they were the first to invite me to London. It would have looked a little strange on my part and so had I to refuse. I am very glad that you are going to play my Concerto with Richter and thank you for your kindness. Some English papers wrote about Joachim that his intonation is somewhat faulty and that he scrapes. What do you say to that? Write me when you are back in Prague.

Greetings from

Dvořák.

František Ondříček see 62. The Choral Society "Hlahol" in Plzeň performed "Stabat Mater" under Dvořák's direction on April 6th and 7th 1884.—Although Dvořák's Violin Concerto is dedicated to Joachim, this artist is not known ever to have played it in public.

7. Facsimile of a page from the manuscript score
of "Stabat Mater".

8. The Czech violin virtuoso, František Ondříček.

75. DVOŘÁK'S FAVOURITE SUMMER RESIDENCE

The Master's first retreat at Vysoká by Příbram, where he always spent the holidays with his family, was an ordinary walled granary behind the villa in the woods where the Count Kaunitz used to keep his carriages, sledges etc. Only when it became known that Dvořák intended to spend the summer there was the place quickly adapted for living quarters. Often he would point to his first summer house and say: "Look there, that's where I worked at 'The Spectre's Bride'."

Later, when the Master had a larger family, he bought from his brother-in-law, the Count Kaunitz, a big place known as "The Sheepfold" from which there is a lovely view of the near-by village of Třebsko. He fenced the place in, built a small one-storeyed house in the middle and laid out a lovely large garden round the house. Here he spent many happy holidays in the circle of his family, whom he loved above everything, and created many beautiful works.

The Master was fond of going to church in Třebsko or Bohutín and played the organ at mass. Best of all he liked to accompany the congregation singing and often used to say that a hymn sung by the people is far better than a badly performed mass sung in the choir. His favourite was the hymn to the Virgin "A Thousand Times we greet Thee". This he loved to play and more than once remarked to the choirmaster in Bohutín, Mr. Peták: "You know, in Prague they don't sing as they do here. They sing, too, but it's not the same thing. Here the people are still a little religious."

Bohumil Fidler: "Recollections of Antonín Dvořák."—*Bohumil Fidler* (1860—1944), composer, choirmaster and choir director in Příbram, a town well-known as a place of pilgrimage and for its ancient silver mines. Near this town is situated the village of *Vysoká*, of which most of the inhabitants are Příbram miners. The estate, with a mansion house, a farm and woods, was the property, in the years 1873-1907, of Dvořák's brother-in -law, Count *Václav Kounic* (1848-1913), whose wife Josefina (1849-1895) was the sister of Dvořák's wife and at one time a very popular actress at the Czech Theatre in Prague. The Dvořáks were at first guests of the Kounices but in 1884 bought a fairly large piece of land and a little house as described above.—*"The Spectre's Bride"*: Dvořák's ballad for solo voices, choir and orchestra (see also 78).—*Třebsko, Bohutín*, villages in the neighbourhood of Vysoká.

76. COUNTRY PLEASURES

Vysoká, 13. 5. 1884.

Dear Friend,

I have been here again for some days now in the loveliest woods where I am spending the most wonderful days in the love-liest weather and am filled with ever new admiration as I listen to the enchanting song of the birds. That in doing so I never think of composing—for that you must take my word, even though it seems unlikely, as most composers are inspired to work by the singing of birds and in listening to them the loveliest melodies occur to them—but I give myself up entirely to the enjoyment and work only when I feel rested and have gained new strength. Don't laugh at me for wanting once to write poetically, but it is such a lovely morning today—indescribably lovely! And the thought that here in this solitude I shall at last have my own piano—I bought it in Prague for my own money and now I am going with John and a big waggon to fetch it from Příbram—all this makes me terribly talkative so that I have left the most im-portant thing to the end. Well, I received the money and music (very *little* of both); I hope you will do better next time.

... Vienna wants an opera from me, as Hanslick writes—they can have one as far as I am concerned, but that the gentle-men do not want "Dimitri" I can't understand and they will be sorry for it yet!

With kindest regards,

Dvořák.

Dvořák to Simrock in Berlin.—Re Vysoká see 75.—The opera "The Peasant a Rogue" was performed in Vienna on Nov. 19th 1885.

77. BIRDS – THE REAL MASTERS

Master Dvořák was also a great lover of singing birds. At home and in the garden arbour at Vysoká he used to have a great many cages with songsters, mostly thrushes, and always when they sang he would say to me: "Do you hear them? How they sing! *They* are the real masters!"

One beautiful summer evening we were walking through the park behind the Count's villa. We had gone beyond the pond into the woods. All the song-birds of the forest, as if at a word of command, started their evening concert. The Master, affected, sat down on a bench and said: "Sit down, comrade, and listen: it is divinely beautiful!" And with deep emotion added: "You know, before I die, I shall write a fine bird symphony and I shall put my very best into it!"

B. Fidler: Recollections of Ant. Dvořák. See 75.

78. "THE SPECTRE'S BRIDE"

Vysoká, 8. 7. 84.

Dear Friend,

I got your letter yesterday, Monday, and it gave me great pleasure. I am also very glad that you have got to Sychrov at last and able to enjoy the country as I am doing here. I feel very happy now especially as my new work "The Spectre's Bride" is making good progress; this week I plan to have the sketch quite completed and then the rest will go smoothly. I thank God that this time, too, my guardian spirit has not forsaken me, and how could it be otherwise when I love him so?

I think (and you will see that I am not deceiving myself) that this work will surpass all my previous works in every respect, not excepting Stabat. Only please don't say anything about it to anybody, it would look like self-praise and I shouldn't want that—you know me. People who have no sense, no nose, no ears, to them I should never say anything like that; but to you I say everything just as my feeling and understanding dictate. But enough of that!

Of the honour shown me in London you know, and I thank you for your congratulations.

You ask me when I am coming to Sychrov. Maybe soon. I shan't begin with the instrumentation in any case till I have had a little breathing-space.

I am longing to see you and looking forward, like the girl in my "Ballad" to her beloved, when she sings:

"I, sad and forlorn, had a lover,
His life than my own was dearer,
Gone is he now across the sea,
Nor has he yet returned to me."
And so God keep you and think sometimes of
Your Friend
Ant. Dvořák.

Dvořák to A. Göbl (see 33) at Sychrov.—The sketch for the ballad "The Spectre's Bride" for solo voices, choir and orchestra, based on the text of the ballad of the same name by *Karl Jaromír Erben* (1811-1870), was written between May 26th and June 16th, and scored between the 24th of the same month and November 27th 1884. It is the story of a girl who, having wished an impious wish, experiences a terrible night with her lover's ghost and is, in the long run, saved by a sincere confession of her guilt. For the performance of the work in Birmingham see 87—90 below.—Distinction received in London: the Philharmonic Society made Dvořák an honorary member of the Society.—The four verses quoted from the Ballad are accompanied in the letter by Dvořák's melody.

79. DVOŘÁK'S SECOND VISIT TO ENGLAND

At Dover we were met by Dvořák's London publisher, Littleton, proprietor of the old and famous publishing firm of Novello, Ewer & Co., and he drove us to his lovely, you might say, royally appointed villa in Sydenham not far from the Crystal Palace. This gigantic building of glass and iron was the first place we went to see and then followed the other sights of the huge city on the Thames. At Littleton's house we made the acquaintance of a noted American composer and a very interesting character: the American composer, Dudley Buck, who invites Dvořák to go on a concerts tour to America. Dudley Buck studied at the Conservatoire in Leipzig and is a great admirer of Dvořák. Whenever he heard that Dvořák was coming to London, he put off, because of him, his departure to his home country. At first Dvořák did not appear very keen on the long journey to America, but now he seems all at once to have taken to the idea and if the conditions are attractive enough, America will see our composer.

This year's festival in Worcester to which the Master was invited is the hundred and sixty-first in the series. Worcester is celebrating this time, with its faithful supporters from Gloucester and Hereford, the octocentenary of the founding of its cathedral, which can accommodate a congregation of 5000.

Thursday was a great day for our Master. Not till you hear it under the venerable vault of a cathedral such as that of Worcester do you feel and experience that inexpressible impression which shakes a man's whole being to the very depths of his soul when there sounds forth the noble beauty which emanates from Dvořák's Stabat Mater. "There is no other work of modern times in the sphere of sacred music which can compare with Stabat"–this is the opinion expressed by all English musical critics: Huefer, Benett, Prout, the critics of the Standard, and of the Worcester, Birgmingham, and Manchester papers into which circles I have been introduced through Dvořák. The rendering was excellent, choir and orchestra were perfectly sure of themselves and the soloists—Albani, Patey, Lloyd and Santley— had a perfect command of the oratorio style, as, in fact, English singers are unrivalled in this field. The work, admirably performed under the firm, confident baton of our Master, made a deep impression on all present. Equally successful was a spirited performance of Dvořák's D major Symphony at an evening concert given in the Public Hall where this splendid work was the high point of a full and varied programme.

I look back on all that we have experienced here as on a

marvellous and beautiful dream. I have witnessed enthusiasm such as I should never have expected of the seemingly cool English—not perhaps some superficial enthusiasm, but understanding and proper appreciation such as Dvořák at home has, generally speaking, so far not been accorded.

V. J. Novotný (see 2): "With Dvořák in England." On Dvořák's second visit to England, he was accompanied by V. J. Novotný when he attended, at the beginning of September 1884, the Musical Festival held to celebrate the eighth centenary of the founding of the magnificent cathedral of Worcester. He conducted Stabat Mater in the Cathedral on Thursday the 11th September in the forenoon, and then, at the concert in the Public Hall, his D major Symphony with the London Philharmonic Orchestra.— *Dudley Buck* (1839-1909): an American composer of sacred music, organist and conductor in Brooklyn.—*Emma Albani* (1852-1930): the artist's name of the famous English soprano L. C. Lajeunesse.

80. DVOŘÁK TO HIS WIFE

Worcester, 12/9 Friday morning, 1884.

Dear Anna,

Yesterday I again had a great day. Stabat Mater, in the wonderful and very large church (4000 people) made a tremendous impression. It was the finest day of the whole celebrations as everybody here was saying. When we left the church, everybody was looking at me and everybody would have liked to shake hands and say a few words, which of course was not possible with such a large number of people. I was then introduced to Lord Compton, and *his lady* then presented me, in a magnificent suite of rooms, to all the élite of beautiful ladies whereupon we went in to breakfast.—There were about 300 people.

Everywhere I appear, whether in the street or at home or even when I go into a shop to buy something, people crowd round me and ask for my autograph. There are pictures of me at all the booksellers' and people buy them only to have some memento.

Yesterday there was the Symphony. I was received with great enthusiasm; then a deputation came to me headed by the Mayor and Lord Compton to express their thanks for my participation in the Worcester Festival. In short, a great victory. God bless you!

Your Antonín.

81. ON THE NEW SYMPHONY (I)

Dear Sir,

First of all my warm thanks for the excellent smoked meats which we enjoyed immensely. Be so good as to forgive me for not having thanked you sooner but I have had a very great deal to do.

Now I am occupied with my new symphony (for London) and wherever I go I have nothing else in mind but my work which must be such again as to make a stir in the world, and God grant that it may! I have sent the "Spectre's Bride" to its destination. The first performance is to be in Plzeň at the beginning of April, then in Olomouc and, on St. John's, in Prague.

Wishing you and your family a merry Christmas and a happy New Year,

With loving greetings, Yours

Antonín Dvořák.

Prague, December 22nd 1884.

Dvořák to Antonín Rus in Mirovice.—A. Rus, judge in Mirovice near Vysoká and one of Dvořák's dearest friends.—The new Symphony for London: the D minor, op. 70, one of the greatest products of Dvořák's genius — a work in which manly resolve and passionate longing lead at last to victorious determination; it was composed between the middle of December 1884 and the 17th March 1885. On the manuscript of the score: "Composed for the Philharmonic Society in London." For the first performance in London see 83 and 84.—The cantata—"The Spectre's Bride" — was given its first performance by the choral society "Hlahol" in Plzeň, with Dvořák conducting, on March 28th 1885.

82. ON THE NEW SYMPHONY (II)

... Today I have just finished the second movement *Andante* of my new Symphony, and am again so happy and contented in my work as I have always been and, God grant, may always be, for my slogan is and shall be:

God, Love and Country! And that alone can lead to a happy goal....

Dvořák to A. Göbl (see 33) at Sychrov, 31. XII. 1884.—Symphony in D minor see 81.

83. NEW PLANS FOR ENGLAND

Praha 18 17/3 85.

Honoured Friend,

I am glad to have news of you again. I often thought that you must have quite forgotten me. As regards the new compositions, I should like, as I wrote in my last, to recommend the big dramatic overture—"The Hussite" and the Scherzo capriccioso, both for large orchestra. I presented both works last year at St. James's Hall and the Crystal Palace in London and now I am writing for the Philharmonic Society in London a new symphony which I must conduct myself on April 22nd of this year. I would gladly give you it, but it will hardly be possible as I must send the score and parts to Berlin straight away where they must be engraved over the summer to be ready for the coming season. I hope we shall see each other in London or perhaps at the Birmingham Festival for which I have written a big work for choir and orchestra. And now I have a great request. You perhaps know what an immense success my Stabat Mater achieved in London and Worcester; I think you need only say the word and it will be possible for Vienna to hear it. So if at any time you should want to present a new work, do not forget about my Stabat Mater.

With heartiest greetings and kind regards,
I remain, Your ever grateful

Ant. Dvořák.

Dvořák to Richter in Vienna.—For the performance of the "Hussite" overture in London see note 69.—The new symphony for the Philharmonic Society in London: D minor, op. 70, see 81 and 84.—The vocal and orchestral work for the Birmingham Festival: the cantata, "The Spectre's Bride", see 84 and 93—96.—Stabat Mater in Worcester see 79. Richter performed this work in Vienna with the Gesellschaft der Musikfreunde, but not till February 19th 1888.

84. MORE ABOUT ENGLAND

Dear Friend,   Plzeň (Pilsen), 18 25/3 85.

Your letter reached me in Plzeň where I have been staying since the 23rd. Yesterday was the first rehearsal with orchestra alone and I was very surprised and delighted that everything was so well prepared and that all sang with great love and enthusiasm. I hope that it will be the same with you, too, in Olomouc.

One thing, however, is worrying me very much and that is that on the day you write of as fixed it is scarcely likely that I shall manage to be with you. It is very distressing for me but when I tell you how matters stand I am sure you will realize that there is no other possibility. I have already written to London that I cannot possibly stay any longer than the end of April. They, however, wish without fail that I should, in addition to my Symphony (on the 22nd), also conduct my Piano Concerto at the 5th Philharmonic Concert—and then not till May 13th *"The Heirs of the White Moutain"* in the Albert Hall.

I am awaiting their answer and so I do not know what the outcome will be. In any case I shall insist that I cannot prolong my stay beyond the 6th May so that I should be in Prague again by the 10th or 11th. But of what use is it when I must be present at rehearsals in Prague where they are to give "The Spectre's Bride" on St John's Day.

As soon as I get word from London I shall let you know. In the meantime I am,

With kindest regards, Your devoted

Antonín Dvořák.

Dvořák to Vicar Geisler in Olomouc in Moravia. — P. Jindřich Geisler (1849-1927), vicar, later canon and dean of the Olomouc cathedral chapter of Olomouc in Moravia, was for many years the President of the musical and choral society "Žerotín" in Olomouc and contributed not a little to its artistic development. He was on very friendly terms with Dvořák, who several times conducted his compositions on their performance by "Žerotín" in Olomouc. The cantata, "The Spectre's Bride", after its first performance in Plzeň (see 81), was given in Olomouc at the beginning of May and by the choral society "Hlahol" in Prague on the 16th of the same month in 1885. As is apparent from the letter, Dvořák did not conduct at these concerts as he was again in London from the middle of May where he conducted the first performance of his D minor Symphony, op. 70 (see 81), with the Philharmonic Society on April 22nd in St. James's Hall, his Piano Concerto in G minor, op. 33, with the pianist Franz Rummel, on May 6th, and "The Heirs of the White Mountain" on May 13th. For this reason the cantata was conducted in Olomouc by Dvořák's friend, Karel Bendl (see 16).

85. LONDON PREMIÈRE OF THE D MINOR SYMPHONY

London, 18 24/4 85.
Westwood House, Sydenham.

Dear Friend,

I was greatly surprised and delighted to get your letter for which my hearty thanks. Before this letter reaches Mirovice you will perhaps know how things here turned out. Splendidly, really splendidly. This time, too, the English again welcomed me as heartily and as demonstratively as always heretofore. The Symphony was immensely successful and at the next performance will be a still greater success.

90

Some extracts from the press notices have probably already appeared in the Czech dailies. Although I have everything I could wish for here, still I would rather be at Vysoká so that I might see and take a delight in the lovely things with which you have beautified our garden.

The weather has been lovely so far, but a change has set in and I am afraid it will last a while, which happens very frequently in England. Hawthorns, and the tree in the gardens—all in the loveliest flower. Roses, violets, to be seen everywhere! Here everything is at least a month earlier. I hope that when I come to you I may see everything once more. Please write to me! For the present I send my warmest greetings to all.

Ever your

Ant. Dvořák.

Dvořák to Ant. Rus (see 81) at Mirovice.

86. DISCORD BETWEEN DVOŘÁK AND SIMROCK

Dear Friend Simrock,

Prague, 18. 5. 85.

I received your letter in London but I was so occupied, and I thought, too, that there was no great hurry.—But now to the point. I fully recognize the validity of the points you put forward, that is, from the business point of view. I, again, from mine, must draw attention to important considerations which I am sure you will also respect.

1. If I give you the Symphony for 3000 M, then I have as good as lost 3000 M—because another firm offers me this sum—in which case I should be extremely sorry if you should wish to force me, so to speak, into such a situation.

2. I think that even though such large works do not produce the desired financial effect straight away, the time may come when everything will be amply made up for, and

3. I beg you to consider that in my Slavonic Dances you have found a gold mine which cannot be so easily underrated, and

4. if you take and consider all that you indicated in your last letter from a common-sense point of view, then we reach a very simple conclusion: not to write symphonies and large vocal and instrumental works, but only publish here and there some songs, piano pieces or dances and I know not what all: this, as an artist who wants to make his mark, I cannot do.

Yes, my Friend, you see that is how I look upon it from my artistic point of view, and I hope you will appreciate mine as I do yours. This, however, does not lead to any conclusion. If you do not wish, or, rather, if you simply cannot give me these 6000 M, then all talking and writing comes to an end; what difference is it between you and me if you have 3000 M less and I by so much more. Remember, I pray you, that I am a poor artist and the father of a family and do not wrong me.

With warm greetings,
Your sincere friend
Ant. Dvořák.

Dvořák to Simrock (see 22) in Berlin.—Here Dvořák replies to a letter in which Simrock is unwilling to go beyond a fee of 3000M for the D minor Symphony, complaining of the high costs and the small sale of large compositions for orchestra. At the same time he expresses the wish that Dvořák should write a new series of "Slavonic Dances" (see 39).

87. BIRMINGHAM PERFORMANCE OF "THE SPECTRE'S BRIDE" IN PROSPECT

Reverend Sir,   Vysoká, 25/7 85.

Your letter gave me great pleasure and I thank you most warmly for your kind invitation. As soon as I can, I shall come to see you. When that will be I cannot say exactly. By August

15th I am to be in London, when the rehearsals for "The Spectre's Bride" will be starting. If it should not be possible before then, I shall at least write you from Birmigham how it came off. In any case, I shall make every effort to come and see you. You know how I have taken the Moravians to my heart and how I love you all, and especially you, my beloved friend.

In the meantime my wife joins with me in sending warmest greetings and kind regards.

Adieu!

I am, Entirely Yours,

Antonín Dvořák.

Dvořák to Vicar Geisler (see 84) in Olomouc.—For the performance of "The Spectre's Bride" in Birgmingham see 88—90.

88. "THE SPECTRE'S BRIDE" AT BIRMINGHAM

Dear Friend,   18 11/8 85.

My wish to write you before my departure for England was not fulfilled though not entirely through my fault. I wanted to visit you on the return journey from the Brno celebrations, but as I should not have been allowed to conduct the "Military Music" at the concert—I stayed at home. According to the law, no *civilian* except the bandmaster may conduct a military band. And I said to myself: And a good thing, too! At least I shall escape the delectation of listening to my works in uniform and in a higher military pitch. Ondříček played my Violin Concerto, and then there was also the I. Rhapsody and the "Tyl" overture.

So I am leaving on Saturday, this time alone, and I don't know how I shall manage. Of course I shall write to you from London about how things go in Birmingham.

I am curious how it will turn out. Gounod is *said* to be coming. I shall then look upon the creator of sweet melodies such as:

93

con amore

Oh how I am looking forward to it.–When I come back (D. V.), I shall come and see you for sure. You have no idea how glad I shall be to see you again! Now if an *order* were to come from England that no *Czech* is allowed to conduct there, how I should rejoice. Well, enough for just now. My head is full of all sorts of worries with this journey of mine.

With greetings to You and All at Sichrov,

Your devoted

Ant. Dvořák.

Dvořák to Göbl at Sychrov. — Dvořák went to England for the fourth time in the middle of August 1885 in order to conduct a performance of "The Spectre's Bride" (see 78) at the *Birgmingham Musical Festival.* Soloists were Albani (soprano, see 79), Josef Maas (tenor) and Charles Santley (baritone). The work was a decided success.— The French composer *Charles Gounod*, from whose opera "Faust and Margarete" the melody is quoted, then called off his attendance at the Festival.

89. DVOŘÁK AT THE SEASIDE

7. Victoria Mansions,

Dear Friend,   West Brighton. 18 19/8 85.

So here I am! having arrived safely on Monday the 17th August at 6 a. m. (*alone this time*). London was still asleep, everything quiet and not a soul in the streets.

I was quite done up by the journey and the same afternoon I had to go to Birmingham where there was a rehearsal in the evening of "The Spectre's Bride". It turned out splendidly, everything just as I would have liked it. The choir is 500 strong and had it studied to the last semiquaver. Before the rehearsal and after I was given a rousing welcome both by the choir and by the public. The next morning I returned to London and today I am

94

writing you again from somewhere else–the lovely seaside town of Brighton to which the wealthiest London class go in summertime. The lovely view of the sea from my room, the sight of thousands of people swarming everywhere, the lovely English women bathing *(and publicly)*, there again *men* and *children*, then a countless number of boats large and small, or here a band playing Scottish folk-songs and goodness knows what else besides: everything is enchantingly lovely so that nobody who has seen it can ever forget it.

Here Novello, too, has a lovely house where I am staying and where, God be praised, I am very content and often call you to mind.

Tomorrow again to London where I have a rehearsal with the orchestra (150 members), on Friday back to Birmingham where I shall stay till the end of the Festival and then (D. V.) I shall travel via Dover, Calais,–Kolín, Frankfurt, Písek, Mirovice–, where my wife will meet me (and where I hope I may see you, too), and the rest I shall tell you when I come. In the meantime may all good attend you and greet from me all your friends, and with a warm handshake from

Your

Ant. Dvořák.

Dvořák to Ant. Rus (see 81) at Mirovice. — See 88.

90. BIRMINGHAM'S WELCOME

Birmingham,

Dear Friend,   Friday evening 10 p. m. 21/8 85.

I am here in this immense industrial town where they make excellent knives, scissors–springs, files and I don't know what else, and besides these music, too. And how well. It's terrible what the people here manage to do and to stand!–There will be 8 concerts in all and each will last 4–5 hours. My day is Thursday the 27th at 8 p. m. Please think of me!

I am looking forward to it immensely. The choir and orchestra are first-class. 100 sopranos, 100 contraltos, 100 tenors, 100 basses and even more, 40 violins, 16 double-basses, 16 cellos and the wind instruments doubled. Just imagine what it will sound like when they start... The Birmingham papers gave me a very warm welcome and the London papers write, too, that my composition is likely to arouse the greatest interest and have the best reception. Maybe it will and maybe it won't! We shall see! And anyhow you will read about it!–

The aria number two (A flat major) for soprano, and number sixteen (G flat major) evoked tremendous enthusiasm both in the orchestra and among the audience. Albani sings straight to the heart that it's a joy to listen to.

I wish you could attend a performance of The Spectre's Bride here; I can't tell you what an impression it made on me. A thousand pities that you are not here!

I want to be home again about the 1st September. This time I am travelling alone, as I wanted to see how it would be. Well, it was all right but the journey (48 hours) is terribly tiring. I must finish. I am going to bed. May all go well with you and don't forget

Your friend

A. Dvořák.

Dvořák to A. Göbl at Sychrov.

91. A FATHER'S PRIDE

Honoured Sir,

The next day, the 8th, I received Your letter and the sum of 25 fl. from my Son and thank You very warmly for the kindness shown me and be so good, Sir, and whisper in his ear that I thank him very much and that I was very anxious about him

96

9. Hans Richter.

WIEN, WÄHRING, COTTAGE
Sternwartestrasse 56.

1. Nov: 1882.

My dear friend!

Would you be kind enough
to accept my invitation to
be my guest during your stay in
Vienna? — You would do me
a great favour. You will find
a quite comfortable chambre
and you will not be disturbed
at all. Please to send me
a consenting Postcard.
Ever yours truly
Hans Richter

10. Letter from Hans Richter to Dvořák.

whether he was not there when there was the train collision outside London on the 23rd, till I read on the 27th August that
he had been in England since the 20th and then I was as if
born again. And ask him, I pray You, Sir, if all the fame is still
ringing in his ears as the papers were writing. Then I have one
more request, Sir, and that is when You speak to my Son if You
would say a word to him to take a day off to visit me in Kladno
and give me the joy of seeing him once again. I hope he will
do so to please You, and I thank You, once again, Honoured Sir,
for your kindness.

Yours very respectfully,

František Dvořák.

At Kladno, the 9th September 1885.

František Dvořák (see 62 and 75) to Dr. J. Zubatý (see 8) in Prague.

92. DVOŘÁK TO HIS PUBLISHER, H. LITTLETON

My dear Friend,

I am arrived quite well to my home.

The verry merry days of Birmingham ar over and naw stay
I agin quiet alone as before. Daily I am walking in the beutyful
forsts and reflecting about Ludmila. Many thanks for the reviev-
ing Coppys of the Oratoris and Cantatas.

The Editor of the Graphic in London asked me for my
Portrait, but I am sorry not to have one.

Please will you be so kind and send him an photgraphy
from Birmingham, supposed they are ready.

Another time something more.

My best compliments fo your family.

God bye, yours sincerely

Ant. Dvořák.

The letter dated 10. IX. 1885 is reproduced in the original English. As is evident
from the spelling, Dvořák picked up English mainly by ear.

93. DVOŘÁK'S NATIONAL CONVICTIONS

... Do not laugh at my Czech brothers and do not be sorry for me either. What I asked of you was only a wish, and if you cannot fulfil it I am justified in seeing in it a lack of goodwill on your part such as I have not found either among English or French publishers. It is evident that you have no idea of the circumstances in which I live.

Dvořák to Simrock in Berlin, 22. VIII. 1885.—In this and the following letter, Dvořák replies to letters in which Simrock ironically makes light of Dvořák's urgent demand for his compositions to be printed also with Czech titles.

94. DVOŘÁK DEFENDS CZECH CULTURAL CLAIMS

Your last letter with national-political comments I found very entertaining; I only regret that you are so badly informed. That is how all our enemies or, more exactly: some individuals *must* write in the intentions and according to the tendency of this or that political paper. But what have *we two to do with politics*; let us be glad that we can dedicate our services to art. And let us hope that nations which possess and represent *art* will never perish, no matter how small they are. Forgive me but I only wanted to say to you that an artist has also his country in which he must have firm faith and for which he must have an ardent heart...

Dvořák in Vysoká to Simrock in Berlin, 10. IX. 1885.—See 92.

95. DVOŘÁK'S PATRIOTISM

Dvořák was a Czech with every breath he breathed, though any kind of "huzza patriotism" was very much against the grain. Dvořák was born on Czech soil of Czech parents and was and remained a Czech because, with his straightforward nature, utterly devoid of all deception, it was not possible for him to cease being a Czech. And even though in following his profession he left Bohemia for a time, his heart remained in his country to which he soon and gladly returned. And yet there could have been nothing easier for a man who, in fact, achieved full recognition abroad sooner than at home, whose art gained him entry to all countries (with the exception perhaps of some Slav lands), whose art itself was international, than to grow lukewarm in his national consciousness. If this had happened, Dvořák would not have been the first nor the last. But that was just not possible. Dvořák could not cease to be a Czech just as he could not cease to be a human being or an artist. It is interesting and instructive that the same Dvořák who, at home, was a sworn opponent of all extravagant radicalism, was unable to appear abroad as anything other than a Czech, heart and soul. Allow me to quote in this connection a reminiscence from the time of my personal contact with Dvořák. In 1885 I accompanied Dvořák to London where he conducted the first performance of the D minor Symphony and, in addition, the Piano Concerto and the Hymnus "The Heirs of the White Mountain". On his arrival in London, Dvořák was surprised to see placards announcing that "Herr Anton Dvořák" was to conduct a new symphony on such and such a day. Dvořák immediately saw to it that on the placards he should be given the Czech designation, "Pan Antonín Dvořák". The club of German artists invited him that time to an evening to be held in his honour, such as had been previously arranged for Bülow, Richter and others, but Dvořák declined giving as his reason that he was not a German artist.

Jos. Zubatý (see 8): from the study "From Recollections of Ant. Dvořák".—For concerts in London see 84.

96. WORK ON SAINT LUDMILLA

Beloved Friend,

I am in the throes of work on my big composition, Saint Ludmilla, and have nothing else in my thoughts so that I have no time left for other things. This composing is a terrible business before you get down to it, and what a lot of thinking over and study it requires. But God grant as soon as I get settled a little I shall come to see you. And how have you got used to your new surroundings? Are you not homesick for Mirovice?

Au revoir very soon! A thousand greetings to you All, Entirely yours,

Antonín Dvořák.

Dvořák at Vysoká to Rus in Písek, 23. IX. 1885.—Ant. Rus see 81.

97. THE NEW SERIES OF "SLAVONIC DANCES", I.

You will forgive me but I simply have not the slightest inclination now to think of such light music. I must tell you that it will not be by any means so simple a matter with the Slavonic Dances as it was the first time. To do the same thing twice is devilishly difficult. As long as I am not in the right mood for it, I cannot do anything. It's something that cannot be forced...

Dvořák at Prague to Simrock in Berlin, 1. I. 1886.—See note on 86.—For composition of a second series of "Slavonic Dances" see 100.

98. THE NEW SERIES OF "SLAVONIC DANCES", II.

Dear Friend Simrock,   Prague, 4. 1. 86.

We arranged in Karlovy Vary that I would send you the "Slavonic Dances" in summer, not before, and so I cannot

understand why you are so indignant now...*You imagine composing as altogether too easy a matter;* it is only possible to start when
we feel *enthusiasm.* But it is difficult to talk about such things,
my dear Friend.

With best greetings,

Your

Ant. Dvořák.

Dvořák to Simrock in Berlin.

99. DVOŘÁK TO SIMROCK ON THE PUBLICATION OF SAINT LUDMILLA BY NOVELLO

Dear Friend Simrock,

Prague 18 16/4 86

I was very much surprised by your letter and that you
should permit yourself such a tone towards me. If you are so
against me then I do not know if I shall be able to create with
joy and enthusiasm. Of what great importance is it if once
I publish, years after, a single work, and in England, too? Is it
perhaps a crime and are you damaged by it? Besides, on my
word of honour, I should not have done so if I had been able
to remember any such written contract, but I swear I know nothing of it. My dear Friend, you are now always casting it up
against me that I ask too high fees, but how am I to provide
for a numerous family (5 children) whose needs are always
growing in connection with their education etc.–how, as an
artist, am I to exist if I am to be dependent on what I earn from
you? I must, as a father, care for a large family, for I have not
only to feed and clothe them but also make provision for their
future, that is I must save for my children in order to ensure
them a proper livelihood, and where am I to get it from? I pray
you, consider all this. I know that you have always meant well
by me, that you have a good and magnanimous heart–there is

no need for me to trouble you with any long explanation, but you will, I am sure, share my point of view. Let me, I beg you, live too, and believe me that it has always been, and is also for the future, my fervent wish that there should be complete harmony between us.

With kind regards, Yours,

Ant. Dvořák.

Dvořák to Simrock in Berlin.—Reply to a letter in which Simrock reproached Dvořák for having given the firm of Novello in London the publication rights for the oratorio "Saint Ludmilla", and citing in that connection a contract dating from the year 1879, according to which he had priority rights for all Dvořák's compositions.— Five children: after Otilie, Anna and Magda, two sons were born to the Dvořáks— Antonín (1883) and Otakar (1885).

100. THE NEW SERIES OF "SLAVONIC DANCES", III.

Dear Friend, Vysoká, 11. 6. 1886.

I have been here at Vysoká for six weeks, and, as the weather is favourable and the country so lovely, I am better off than Bismarck in Varzin, yet at the same time I am far from being idle. I spend most of the day in my garden, which I keep in beautiful order and love as I do "the art divine", and go rambling through the woods. There is not much time for composing but now it is going ahead briskly. I am enjoying doing the Slavonic Dances immensely and am sure that this (the second series) will be quite different (no joking and no irony!). They are not, however, likely to be finished by July 1st, but certainly will be by the 15th, and then there will be time enough as they won't be coming out before September in any case?

More next time, Your

Ant. Dvořák.

Dvořák to Simrock.—*Varzin:* the Prussian village which was the seat of the Bismarck family.—Dvořák at last set to work on the *"Slavonic Dances"*, piano duets, op. 72, which he composed between the beginning of June and the 9th July 1886.

101. DVOŘÁK TO LITTLETON

Vysoká, 22. 8. 86.

My dear Friend,

I am extremely glad to hear from you, you are pleased with taking my wife to London, whaer we will remain till Noveb. 6.

Please don't send the letters to Prague. I seldom stay there and all the letters from Prague send to Vysoká reach me allways one or two days later.

We remain here on Vysoka till 20. of Septber, then we go to Prague. I liwe Prague on Oktober 1. and will be in London 3. or 4. of Octobre. Can you send me a timetabel? and a copy of Ludmila?

Meanwhille
I am always respecthfully yours,

A. Dvořák.

Letter written in English.

102. "SAINT LUDMILLA" IN ENGLAND

London, 18. 10. 86.

Dear Friend,

At last everything is over, my victory was tremendous and I hasten to give you more details.

Saint Ludmilla made in general a great impression and was the high point of the whole festival as all the *London newspapers* write and which you will read in our papers in the next few days. Such a choir and orchestra as is here I have not heard in England yet. It was magnificent. But all words are vain. The welcome I got from the audience, the choir and the orchestra was so hearty and sincere that I was almost carried off my feet.

During the performance, nearly every number was received

with storms of applause and at the end of Part I, the audience, choir and orchestra broke out into such cheers that I felt quite queer.

At the singing of the Aria by Albani "O grant that I may kiss the dust from off thy feet", there was a death-like silence and I was told that people were moved to tears. In short it was most impressive. The choir numbered 350, the orchestra 120, and the best voices and artists. After it ended (it lasted from 11.30 till 3 p. m.), the calls for Dvořák seemed interminable and I had to bow again and again and the whole choir and orchestra waved their handkerchiefs, and finally I said a few words to the audience in English and thanked them for their warm welcome and the excellent performance of my work, which again called forth new storms of applause. In short it was a great day on which I shall always look back with joy...

The weather here is miserable, continual fog and rain—believe me I should be glad to be away from here, but it's no use, duty calls and I must stay till the 6th November and then with all haste—to Prague.

Greetings to You and all Your Friends,

A. Dvořák.

Dvořák to A. Rus in Písek.—The oratorio "Saint Ludmilla" was written for the Musical Festival in Leeds where it was also given its first performance, with Dvořák conducting, on October 15th 1886. This was his fifth visit to England this time accompanied by his wife. The soloists were: again the famous Albani in the part of Ludmilla; the contralto Patey as Svatava; the tenor Lloyd as Bořivoj and the bass Santley as the hermit Ivan. The Sunday Times wrote after the performance as follows: "Our friends of art in the north were very happy to have the celebrated Master for the first time in their midst and, at the same time, very proud that a work of such importance should be first performed at their Festival. The audience had already at the end of the first part of Saint Ludmilla come to the certain conclusion that they had before them a master work and greeted this, and other compositions by the Master, with real ovations. And from that moment the success of the oratorio was assured."—The work was again conducted by Dvořák in London on October 29th and November 6th 1886.

103. SIMROCK AND THE NEW SLAVONIC DANCES

... Now that your Slavonic op. 72 has just come out, I must tell you again how *very* delighted I am with *these splendid* pieces. But–there's no help: they must be orchestrated–they simply shout for it!! And, Donnerwetter! if you don't do it yourself soon I shall have to ask somebody else to–and don't go promising England any more works–I shall confiscate them!!!

Simrock in Berlin to Dvořák in Prague, 21. X. 1886.—The second series of eight "*Slavonic Dances*", op. 72 was originally written, as was the first, as piano duets (see 99). The instrumentation for orchestra was realized by Dvořák in December 1887.—No works for England: see 99.

104. DEDICATION OF "SAINT LUDMILLA"

Dear Friend,   Prague, 18 17/11 86.

Thank you for your kind letter and for your congratulations on the first performance of Ludmilla in England.

I know that all this gives you real pleasure and that you follow my every step with intense interest, and, besides, you and your choral society "Žerotín" have given me so many proofs of your sincere love and favour that I do not know how I could show my gratitude. And so I thought that I should do well if, as an expression of the high and fully merited respect which I have for your truly artistic achievements–there were written at the head of the voluminous score of "Saint Ludmilla" the following:

Dedicated to the Choral Union "Žerotín" in Olomouc

by Antonín Dvořák.

Accept then this gift from me and, at the same time, I wish You and Your Žerotín every success,

Your deeply devoted

Antonín Dvořák.

Dvořák to P. Geisler in Olomouc.—P. J. Geisler and "Žerotín" see 84.

105. AN ACKNOWLEDGEMENT

Prague, 12/2 87.

Dear Friend,

Allow me to thank you for your warm and appreciative notice of Ludmilla in today's N. Listy. Do not be surprised that I do so. An artist who feels and thinks and has learnt something about his craft, and knows that in creating his work he gave his whole soul to it, is always glad when among many, be it only one voice is found of which he can say: "Here is one who has understood me." And this you have done today. For which my warmest thanks.

With the expression of my friendly respect,
I remain, Most sincerely yours,

Antonín Dvořák.

Dvořák to J. B. Foerster see 15.—The letter refers to Foerster's notice of the oratorio "Saint Ludmilla" in the Czech daily, Národní Listy after the performance of the work at the National Theatre in Prague on February 25th 1887.

106. SYMPHONIC VARIATIONS

Prague 18 28/3 87.

Dear and Honoured Friend,

I hear that you are going to London again in May to give one of your concerts and I would take the opportunity to ask you if you would not care to present one or other of my compositions. I am thinking especially of the D minor Symphony which you were good enough to perform this year in Vienna. Should you, however, want only something new, then I would recommend a work which has not yet been published but which will not remain so long if you give it its christening. It is a big piece for orchestra... "Symphonic Variations" which I wrote in 1877 and had performed for the first time in Prague only recently. Hoping that you will consider my suggestion favourably,

I am, Respectfully yours,

Ant. Dvořák.

Dvořák to Richter in Vienna.—The *Symphonic Variations* for large orchestra, on a theme from the choral work "Guslar" for male choir, was completed in September 1877 as op. 40, but was not published till 1877 and then under op. 78, by Simrock. For its performance under Richter in London see 107, 109 and 110.

107. RICHTER AND THE "VARIATIONS"

Vienna, Währing,

Most honoured Friend,   Sternwartegasse 56,

I am a poor overworked man: may that be my excuse to you for not having written to you immediately after the performance of the "Scherzo capriccioso" and the D minor Symphony. Your letter made the general rehearsal of such a bit of rubbish as "Harold" (by our choirmaster Pfeffer) slightly less painful and I am glad to seize the opportunity to come into contact with a musician by Divine grace. I had intended, in any case, before fixing my London programme, to inquire of you whether you had not something for me. Now your Symphonic Variations come as a splendid embellishment of my programme: and so are also accepted with warmest thanks *as certain*. Kindly send me the score *as soon as possible* to the above address, the orchestra parts then to Mr. N. Vert, 6, Cork Street, Burlington Gardens, London W. I should like very much to perform this work at one of my first programmes. The "Scherzo Capriccioso" I have already included in my programme.

How often has the D minor Symphony been performed in London? This work is a great favourite of mine (perhaps my greatest) but I must, out of consideration for the promoters, be careful not to give something that has been frequently heard, though I may say without arrogance, that only a *dramatically* trained conductor, a Wagnerian (Hans Bülow will forgive me) can do *full* justice to this Symphony. Send me a few lines about the number of the *London* performances: on that will depend whether I can perform the work *this* season.

With warmest greetings,

Your ever devoted

Hans Richter.

Richter to Dvořák in Prague.—March 31st 1887 Dvořák's *Scherzo capriccioso,* op. 66 for orchestra was composed between April 6th and May 2nd 1883 and was performed under Richter with the Vienna Philharmonic on Dec. 1st 1886, the D minor Symphony, op. 70, (see 81) on Jan. 16th 1887.

108. DVOŘÁK THANKS RICHTER

Prague, 18 4/4 87.

My dear friend,

I am most thankfull for your last letter, which gave me so much pleasure and I asure you on reading it I was affected to tears. I am fully awere that you are the only man and musician (among so many others), who understands me quite well and to whom I must always be obliged, having done so much for me. I can't but express my feelings of greatest gratitude to you for the kindness in performing my new composition I offered to you. I shall not fail to send you the full score as soon posibel. The orch. part you find in London. As I remember, the Symfonie D minor has been performed only once under my direction at the Filharmonic Concerts 1885 and you can give as much as you please. Repeating manny many thanks to you,

I remain sincerely yours

Ant. Dvořák.

Dvořák to Richter in Vienna.—The letter was written in English. For the first performance of the D minor Symphony in London see 84.

109. RICHTER REQUESTS THE SCORE OF THE "VARIATIONS"

My dear friend,   Währing, 9. April 1887.

Many thanks for your letter. I enjoyed it as a sign of your friendship, and as an instance of your perfect English, too. Please to send the score of the "Symfonische Variationen" as soon as possible.
With kind regards, Yours sincerely,

Hans Richter.

Richter in Vienna to Dvořák in Prague.—Written in English.

110. RICHTER TO DVOŘÁK FROM LONDON

Dearly esteemed Friend,   13. V. 1887.

I come positively carried away by the first rehearsal for the Third Concert at which we are playing your "Symphonic Variations". It is a magnificent work! I am glad to be the first to perform it in London, but why have you kept it back so long?? These Variations can take their place among the best of your compositions. I shall send you news of the performance.
With kindest regards, Yours,

Hans Richter.

They will be on the programme of the next Philharmonic Concerts in Vienna.

The Symphonic Variations were performed by the Philharmonic Society at the Crystal Palace, with Richter conducting, on 15. V. 1887.

111. A LETTER OF THANKS

Dearly esteemed Friend,

Yesterday I received your letter and programme which gave me great pleasure. May Heaven give you thanks for my pen is too weak to put into words what I felt on reading your letter.

And the splendid orchestra! Express, I beg you, a thousand thanks, in my name, to your valiant army! Mr. C. Barry also sent me a few lines which I was delighted to get.

I am here with my family where I shall remain till the end of September. It is a small village with plenty of woods where we lead a quiet and happy life, and it would give me double pleasure if you would once send me a few lines to Vysoká. Once more my warm thanks for your kindness and a hearty hand-clasp from

Your devoted

Ant. Dvořák.

Vysoká by Příbram, Bohemia,
18 23/5 87.

Dvořák to Richter in London.—According to Dvořák's letter to Simrock dated 29. V. 1887, Richter wrote to Dvořák in Prague after the performance of the Symphonic Variations: "Your Symphonic Variations had an enormous success and at the some hundreds of concerts which I have conducted during my life no *new work* has ever had such a success as yours." This letter is Dvořák's reply.—*Charles Ainslie Barry* (1830-1915), an English writer on music and composer who wrote the programme notes, in the form of an analysis of the works performed, for London concerts.

112. DVOŘÁK ON HIS MASS IN D MAJOR

Dear Friend,   Vysoká 18 17/6 87.

I have the honour to inform you that I have successfully concluded my Mass in D major and that I am truly satisfied with it. I think it will be a work which will fully answer its purpose.

110

It would be possible to enumerate: Faith, hope and love to God Almighty and thanks for the great gift of being enabled to bring this work in the praise of the Highest and in the honour of art to a happy conclusion.

Do not wonder that I am so religious. An artist who is not —could not produce anything like this. Have we not examples enough in Beethoven, Bach, Raphael and many others?

And finally my thanks to you for providing the impulse to write the work in such a form, otherwise I should hardly have thought of it; for before this I always wrote works of such a kind on a large scale with a large number of performers. This time the artistic means employed are very modest and yet I dare to assert that the work has turned out well...

My respectful compliments to Yourself and to
Madam, your wife,
                                    Ant. Dvořák.

Dvořák to Josef Hlávka in Prague.—Architect Josef Hlávka (1831-1908), Czech patron of the arts, founder and first president of the Czech Academy of Sciences and Arts. His wife, Zdeňka, was a good pianist and a sincere admirer of Dvořák's music. Hlávka, who held Dvořák in high esteem, asked him to write a mass for the dedication of the chapel on his estate in Lužany in Bohemia (now the property of the Czech Academy of Sciences). Dvořák wrote the Mass in D major, op. 86 (March 26th to June 17th 1887), which was first performed under his direction at the Castle Chapel in Lužany on September 11th 1887. The Mass was originally composed for choir with only organ accompaniment but when the firm of Novello in London later decided to publish it (1893), Dvořák provided the instrumentation for a small orchestra.

113. DVOŘÁK'S PIETY

A characteristic feature of Dvořák's nature was his *piety*, but a sincere piety not asking anybody to deny their own religious views, a piety, which was rooted in his own heart and awakened only respect in everyone who recognized it for what it was. Dvořák's piety was perhaps connected with his love for Nature, and, in Nature, especially with the singing-birds for which he cherished an almost child-like affection. Dvořák was convinced to the depths of his being that over the world there watches a higher power which directs everything for the best: and he was devoted to that power with fervour and gratitude. Not long before Dvořák's death, I was travelling with him by train to Příbram: on the way his attention was attracted by the limestone rocks near Beroun and seeing work there in full swing called forth the observation that these resources, too, would be exhausted in the course of time. I put his fears at rest by saying that even if the whole of Bohemia was exhausted, the Limestone Alps alone would suffice for the whole of Europe. "And who contrived it so?" with which question the conversation concluded. Proof of Dvořák's piety are also his manuscripts, which regularly begin with the date and "With God" and end with the date and "God be thanked"; proof of his piety, too, are Dvořák's sacred compositions, above all one of the most religious works that I know—Stabat Mater. But Dvořák's piety was a piety of the heart, of one who is devoted to God from conviction and not to some particular religious community. The same Dvořák who devoted his art to a text of the Catholic confession glorifies without hesitation in the Hussite Overture the most glorious period of our history when Catholicism was overpowered by Hussitism, and I think nobody would be more surprised than he if anyone should see in that composition a proof of his religious insincerity or lukewarmness.

Dr. Zubatý (see 8) : From "Recollections of Ant. Dvořák".

114. DVOŘÁK TO HANS VON BÜLOW IN BERLIN

Prague, 18 15/10 87.
Žitná ulice 10.

Dear and esteemed Friend,

I hear and read in the papers that you kindly intend to perform at your concerts, probably in Berlin, my Hussite

11. Music publisher Henry Littleton.

12. Littleton's residence in Sydenham.

Overture. It is a new proof of your goodness and friendliness towards me, which I value immensely, and for which I owe you a great debt of thanks—this time, however, I should take the liberty of asking this of you: would it not be possible to perform, in place of the Overture, perhaps my D minor Symphony which has not yet been heard in Berlin? Or is there not perhaps some other work, maybe the Serenade for wind instruments?

I do not in any way wish to insist but, considering that the Philharmonic played it once already with Joachim, I should be glad if you would be so good as to give preference to some other work.

And lastly, I am so bold as to remind you of your kind promise in connection with Dimitri. The opera has been translated by Mrs. M. Kleinschrod-Stieler in Munich and I am expecting to get it very shortly accompanied by a full German text. If you take the fate of my work into your masterly hands, I have no doubt it will go round the world.

With the expression of my deep respect and gratitude,

I remain, Your most devoted

Antonín Dvořák

Hans von Bülow (1830-1894), an eminent German conductor and pianist, was a sincere admirer of Dvořák's music and in Germany frequently performed the Hussite Overture for which he had a particular liking. Dvořák requited him by dedicating to him his Fifth Symphony—the *F major Symphony* from the year 1875, which Simrock first published in 1887 as op. 76 (see 117). *The Philharmonic:* Philharmonisches Orchester in Berlin.

115. HANS BÜLOW REPLIES FROM HAMBURG

Honoured Master,

It would give me great pleasure if I could, in accordance with your wish, perform the D minor Symphony instead of the Hussite Overture.

I am afraid, however, that I shall meet with difficulties:

the concert director, Hermann Wolff, has already accepted for the Philharmonic Concerts a great number of new symphonies, for instance those of Gernsheim, Strauss, Stanford (to be conducted by the authors in person) and the greater part of the public wishes to hear well-known old-classical works. Nevertheless, on my next visit to Berlin I shall try to bring about the change of programme you desire. It would be a great help if your publisher would intervene and make the request directly to concert director Wolff: they both live in the same street etc.

Forgive my haste—I am overwhelmed with rehearsals. I recommended your Dimitri to director Pollini some time ago in the warmest terms (it is in fact the *only* musical drama of more recent date that I suggested to him as being worth producing he, however, (without my having the least idea) has bought Smetana's Dalibor, which will now be given priority. Let us hope that it is merely a matter of postponement.

With the expression of my deep respect,

I remain, Your entirely devoted admirer,

Hans Bülow.

17. X. 1887

See 114.—The D minor Symphony, op. 70, was performed by Bülow with the Berlin Philharmonic on the 27th and 28th October 1889 (see 135).—*Friedrich Gernsheim* (1839-1916) and *Richard Strauss* (1864-1947), German composers, *Sir Charles Villiers Stanford* (1852-1924) an Anglo-Irish composer.—Pollini see 55.—In Hamburg there was no performance of either Smetana's Dalibor or of Dvořák's Dimitri.

116. BÜLOW AND THE "HUSSITE" IN HAMBURG

...The composition which, alongside Smetana's "Tábor", must be considered the most splendid musical embodiment of the Hussite idea, deeply affected the audience through its spiritual power, its unusual originality and its irresistable force of expression, and excited among musicians real enthusiasm. I have yet to see the musicians here in such an ecstasy, and when, after the first part of the programme, that is just after the "Hussite", we met Bülow in the press room, it seemed to me as if we had all just come straight from a Hussite battle, fought to a victorious conclusion, and, with enthusiastic clamour and rejoicing, were crowding round the great commander to pay the tribute of our fervent gratitude and boundless admiration.

Dr. Ludevít Procházka on the Hussite Overture in Hamburg in November 1887.—Dr. L. Procházka (1837-1888), Czech musical critic and writer, an ardent propagator of Bedřich Smetana and Dvořák, was living at this time in Hamburg with his wife, Marta, a noted singer and member of the Hamburg Opera.

117. BÜLOW ACKNOWLEDGES A DEDICATION

Honoured Master,

The dedication from you—along with the composer, Brahms, the most favoured of God of the present time—is a higher distinction than any Grand Cross from any Prince. I accept the honour with the warmest thanks.

Your respectful and devoted admirer,

Hans Bülow.

Hans von Bülow in Hamburg to Dvořák, 25. XI. 1887.—For Dvořák's dedication of the F major Symphony see 113.

118. SIMROCK ON DVOŘÁK

...Amazing what an amount of music that man has in his head, and in spite of—or better because of—his taciturnity (according to his wife they call him in Prague the Czech Moltke) a delightful person! And then he hangs on you with adoring respect and also speaks in that way; he wants to go to Vienna as soon as possible to see you.

Simrock to Brahms in Vienna, 29. X. 1887.—Dvořák's wife was an excellent contralto and sang the solo parts for contralto in some of her husband's oratorios.—Moltke: evidently Count Helmuth B. Moltke, the Prussian Field Marshal.

119. RICHTER INVITES DVOŘÁK TO VIENNA

Vienna, Währing, Cottage,
Sternwartegasse 56.   1. Nov. 1887.

My dear Friend,

Would you be kind enough to accept my invitation to be my guest during your stay in Vienna? — You would do me a great favour. You will find a quite comfortable chambre and you will not be disturbed at all. Please send a consenting Postcard.

Ever yours truly,

Hans Richter.

Reply in English to the letter in which Dvořák thanks him for his readiness to perform the Symphonic Variations and Stabat Mater in Vienna. See also 120.

120. RICHTER'S INVITATION ACCEPTED

Dear Friend,   18 5/11 87.

Many thanks for your kind invitation and I shall be very pleased to stay at your house. I am bringing the Variations with me—the score and parts you had in London. As you have your first Philharmonic Concert on November 13th, I hope there will be a rehearsal on Friday and Saturday when, if it is possible, you could make use of the opportunity to play through the Variations—half-an-hour at the most would do it.

Au revoir then in Vienna.

Your devoted

Ant. Dvořák.

If I arrive in Vienna (Franz Joseph Bahn) at 10 o'clock at night, can I still get a cab to your place in Währing? But I should not like to trouble you so late.

Perhaps I shall come in the afternoon at 3 o'clock (Nordbahnhof) but on what day I cannot say yet. In any case I shall go straight to Währing and seek you out.

Reply to the preceding letter (119).—Dvořák was thus in Vienna twice as Richter did not perform the Variations with the Vienna Philharmonic till December 4th 1887 (121).

121. THE "VARIATIONS" IN VIENNA

...I spent some wonderful hours with Brahms; it was also the only recompense for the tiring journey to Vienna. As Brahms says—and he knows the Viennese public only too well: no composition has ever taken on like the "Variations". The work was magnificently played and the audience was generous with its outspoken praise.

Brahms presented me with a lovely cigar-holder for my "Variations"...

Dvořák to Simrock in Berlin, 6. XII. 1887.—See 120.

...I had a great deal of discussion with Dvořák and am glad that we reached agreement about various things, especially the beginning of the third act (of Jacobin). Dvořák had only one misgiving—that for such an allegory you can only write pleasing, more serious and fey-like music and that a teacher could not write such music; that a teacher can only write something funny and nothing really beautiful and that the moment it is attributed to a teacher it must have a comical character (he thinks it would have to be parodied, which is impossible in an allegory).

I argued that teachers compose also serious works and masses, whereupon he replied: "That's just it, all the masses are funny, I know them." And in short he kept to his point that he can only write an allegory if the remark is omitted that it was composed by a teacher. Stroupežnický, on hearing my discussion with Dvořák, said: "Now at least I have learned something and see that nobody can write a libretto who has not some idea of music." This because Dvořák was saying every little while: you see I need a rhythm like this—and instead of saying an iamb, a trochee or a dactyl etc., he began to whistle a melody or took a piece of paper and jotted down a melody on it. I shall have a lot of work still with the second act in which a number of changes will have to be made. But as long as he does not interfere with the plot and does not spoil the dramatic passages I gladly accommodate him in other things—for they are undoubtedly demands made by the music and must be paid heed to...

Marie Červinková (see 48) to her father, Dr. F. L. Rieger, 8. III. 1888.—After the opera "Dimitri", Červinková wrote the libretto for the opera *"The Jacobin"*, the music for which was not composed till after long delays at the end of the year 1887. The sketch for the opera was begun on the 10th November, the score completed between the 21st March and the 18th November 1888. It is one of Dvořák's most popular operas. The action takes place in a small Czech town at the time of the French Revolution and one of the chief characters is that of the very attractive country teacher-musician.

123. DVOŘÁK'S CREATIVE ABSORPTION

...With the composition he was working on he was usually in love. When he was writing "The Jacobin", he told me with shining eyes that no composer had composed to such a lovely libretto. "There's a village teacher there, a character, I tell you, you could go daft about." In 1896 when he was finishing "The Wild Dove", I met him on Václavské náměstí. He told me what a delightful musical theme it was. "And when the widow goes to the churchyard, the dove coos; the woman is seized with despair and jumps into the water, and the dove coos again." I had never heard him give such a truly lively and epic description...

Ladislav Dolanský (see 73) in his book "Musical Memoirs".—For the composition of the opera "The Jacobin" see 122, and 123; the symphonic poem, "The Wild Dove", op. 110, see 207.

124. THE SOURCES OF DVOŘÁK'S INSPIRATION

One moment always revealed to me as in a flash the secret of his creation. He had not words sharp enough for Škroup's "Kde domov můj"–he would have composed a new Czech anthem–and not long afterwards he is composing the music on Škroup's motifs to "Kajetán Tyl". He is turning over the pages of Berlioz' "Requiem" with every sign of irritation and soon he announces the publication of his own Requiem. I see him with Liszt's Saint Elizabeth, and very soon London is listening to Dvořák's Saint Ludmilla. Only a great composer can follow in the steps of his great predecessors. Was he inflamed by the same exasperation to create his other compositions, his chamber music?

Leoš Janáček (see 14): from the book of "Reminiscences of Antonín Dvořák".—František Škroup (1801-1862), Czech composer and conductor, the author of several operas and the music of the present-day Czech national anthem "Kde domov můj" to words by J. K. Tyl (see 55).

125. WORK ON "THE JACOBIN" CONTINUES

Dearest Friend,   Vysoká, 19/6 88.

...Yesterday I finished the score of Act I and am perfectly satisfied with my work.

I think that this time those who have doubts about my *dramatic talent* will be satisfied if not surprised. Just as "The Spectre's Bride" and Ludmilla are the first among my works (outside the theatre), I think "The Jacobin" will be the first among the operas. You say you are coming to Prague one of these days (about the 20th). I may be going through Prague on Saturday. — I intend to go away somewhere—and at the same time I should like very much to visit you at Sychrov.

Write me a line!

Kind regards from my wife and a special embrace to yourself,

Your sincere friend,

Antonín Dvořák.

Dvořák to A. Göbl at Sychrov.—For the composition of "The Jacobin" see 122.— The country mansion at Sychrov was the property of the Rohan family.

126. "THE JACOBIN"—SATISFACTION

...Early in the morning visitors arrived. Dvořák came with a broad smile which he reserves for occasions when he is in a specially good mood. He had come, he said, to congratulate me as he was not able to come yesterday, and I could not help saying to him that now perhaps he could judge whether the musical critics were right who for so many years discouraged him from composing the libretto...

Marie Červinková in her diary, 13. II. 1889, after the première of the opera "The Jacobin" which took place at the National Theatre in Prague on the 12th February 1889.

127. THE BEGINNING OF A FRIENDSHIP

27th March, 1888.
Vienna.

My dear, good and highly esteemed Friend,

Although it is terribly difficult for me to write in German, I must make use of this *Panslav* language to tell you that I have often thought of you and that I shall never forget how well and kindly you received me in Prague. I stayed for 3¹/₂ weeks in Paris (where my concerts were very successful), then in London where everything went off equally well, and now I am returning to Russia and am only passing through Vienna. Dear Friend, give my kindest regards to Madam, your wife, and allow me to say once more that I am very glad and happy to have won your valued friendship. I hope we may see each other again in November. With a hearty hand-shake,

I remain, Your true friend,

P. Tchaikovsky.

P. S. The orchestra in London is very good and the way these people read from sight is quite amazing. We often spoke of you and your Symphony is awaited with impatience. My hearty greetings to Bendl, Fibich, Kovařovic, Ondříček jun., Neruda, Čech, Anger and all good friends. Au revoir!!!

In 1887, *Peter Iljich Tchaikovsky* (1840-1893) made a concert tour of the town of Western Europe, as a successful conductor of his own works. He was in Prague for the first time in February 1888 when he conducted two concerts. He made Dvořák's acquaintance at an evening held in his honour on February 14th and the day following visited Dvořák at his flat. At a dinner given by the Russian Circle on February 16th, Dvořák replied to the Czech toast of the Russian guest, whereupon Tchaikovsky requited him with an embrace and a reference to "his newest but warmest bond of friendship with the great Czech, Antonín Dvořák."—The impatiently awaited Symphony: in April 1888, August Manns presented Dvořák's F major Symphony in London (see also note to 114).—*Zdeněk Fibich* (1850-1900), *Karel Kovařovic* (1861-1920), noted Czech composers, especially in the sphere of dramatic music. *Ondříček jun.*, i. e. Karel, at that time leader of the orchestra of the Prague National Theatre, brother of František, the violin virtuoso; *Alois Neruda*, violoncellist, *Adolf Čech* (see 9) and *Mořic Anger* (see 12), conductors of the National Theatre orchestra.

Birmingham,
Wednesday, 29th Aug. 1888.

Dear Friend,

Yesterday's performance of "Stabat Mater" was a splendid triumph for your lovely work. Have you something new for me for Vienna? I shall be back on the 4th August.

With kindest regards,

Ever yours truly,

Hans Richter.

Richter in Birmingham to Dvořák at Vysoká.—On August 28th 1888, Richter conducted "Stabat Mater" at the Birmingham Musical Festival.

129. DVOŘÁK TO TCHAIKOVSKY ON "ONEGIN"

Prague, 14/2 January 1889.

Dear Friend,

When you were last here in Prague I promised to write to you about your opera "Onegin". Now not only your request compels me to do so but my inward desire to tell you all that I felt on hearing your work. I confess with pleasure that your opera made a very deep impression upon me—an impression such as I expect from a true work of art, and I do not hesitate to say that none of your compositions has given me such pleasure as Onegin.

It is a splendid work, full of warm feeling and poesy, and, at the same time, worked out to the last detail; in short, this music speaks to us and penetrates so deep into our soul that it is unforgettable. Whenever I go to the theatre I feel as if I were in another world.

I congratulate you and ourselves on this work and pray God you may be spared to give the world many more such compositions.

With a warm embrace,

Your devoted

Antonín Dvořák.

In autumn 1888, Tchaikovsky came to Prague for the second time to conduct another concert of his own works held on November 30th and the Czech première of his opera *"Eugen Onegin"*. It is to this latter event that Dvořák's letter refers.

130. TCHAIKOVSKY THANKS DVOŘÁK

30/18 Jan. 1889.

S. Frolovskoje

Dear, beloved and esteemed Friend,

You cannot imagine how delighted I was with your letter.

I value very highly your opinion of my opera not only because you are a great artist but also because you are a man that is frank and sincere. I am exceedingly proud and happy that I have been able to deserve a sincere word of commendation from you, my dear Friend. I thank you once more from the bottom of my heart.

Forgive me for not answering your letter immediately. In spite of all my efforts to read your letter I could not understand it although I guessed that its content was agreeable. The letter had to be sent to Moscow, to Hřímalý, to be translated and the translation reached me only today.

About ten days ago I sent a letter to A. O. Patera requesting him to discuss with you in detail your journey to Moscow. I have not, however, so far received an answer. I beg you, dear Friend, give your consent and come, it is the great wish of all of us here.

My compliments to Madam, your wife, and to all our mutual friends: Bendl, Fibich, N. P. Apraksin, Marie Federovna etc.

With a warm embrace, dear Dvořák,

Yours,

P. Tchaikovsky.

Written in Russian.—*Jan V. Hřímalý* (Grzhimali) (1844-1915), teacher of violin at the Czarist Conservatoire in Moscow and leader of the Moscow Symphony orchestra.—
Adolf Patera (1836-1912), librarian of the Czech Museum in Prague and an ardent promoter of Czecho-Russian relations.

131. TCHAIKOVSKY INVITES DVOŘÁK TO RUSSIA

Leipzig, 1. March 89.

My dear Friend,   17. February

A. O. Patera informs me that you are willing to conduct a concert next season in Moscow. You have no idea how delighted I was with this news.

Thank you, dear Friend. You are doing our Moscow Musical Society a great honour and I am sure that Moscow will know how to return thanks.

Now it is necessary, however, to settle two questions:

1. The time of your arrival and
2. the remuneration for your work.

Our concerts are fixed for the following days:

1889	November	. . . . .	2. 9. 23. (new mode)
	December	. . . . .	7. 21.
1890	January	. . . . .	11. 18.
	February	. . . . .	7. 14. 21. 28.
	March	. . . . .	4.

Be so good as to let us know which of the suggested days suits you best.

Such an excellent and outstanding artist as you are should be paid for his trouble with heaps of gold. As it is, the resources of our Society are not so ample as to be able to give you a fee such as the greatness of your name would call for. We could offer you only about 800 roubles (about 1000 gulden) to defray your travelling expenses.

Be kind enough, dear Friend, to send me an answer to these two questions as soon as possible. Address it to Wolf (Berlin W. 19 am Carlsbad).

If you write in Czech, then please ask our mutual friend, A. O. Patera, to enclose a translation.

I was very sorry not to meet you in Dresden.

With kind regards to your Wife,

Your sincerely affectionate friend,

P. Tchaikovsky.

Written in Russian.—A. O. Patera see 130.—Tchaikovsky's invitation to Dvořák to hold concerts in Russia was accepted. Dvořák was in Russia in March 1890 and conducted a concert of the Tsarist Musical Society in Moscow on the 11th March and a concert in Petrograd on the 22nd March (see 136).—*Wolff:* the Berlin concert director Hermann W.—On the 13th March 1889, Dvořák conducted a concert of the Dresden Philharmonic Orchester (F major Symphony, Nocturno op. 40 and the II. Slavonic Rhapsody).

132. NEW COMPOSITIONS FOR PIANO

Dearest Friend,   Vysoká, 14/6 89.

I have been at Vysoká since the 6th May and have not been to see you yet! It is terrible! But what's to be done when I am not as I used to be. To travel—what a delight it was for me formerly—and now? I am glad when I can sit at home. But, again, my longing to see you is greater and greater and so I think I shall be visiting you shortly. I have just finished writing 13 compositions for piano solo. An ominous number, but that was the number of the Moravian Duets, too, and yet they have gone round the world quite a bit. Perhaps it will come off again. I have a journey to Berlin in connection with them and if I return the following week via Leipzig, Cheb and Plzeň, I shall look in and see you. Goodbye for the present, and au revoir!

Your affectionate friend,

Antonín Dvořák.

Dvořák to A. Rus in Písek (see 81).—13 compositions: the cycle—*Poetic Tone-Pictures* for pianoforte, op. 85, composed between the 17th April and the 6th June 1889.—The proposed journey to Berlin fell through owing to illness in Dvořák's family.

133. AN OFFER DECLINED

Dear Sir,

Permit me to inform you that after carefully weighing all considerations, I am unable to decide to accept this high post at the Prague Conservatoire, and certainly not least because I am afraid that I should not be able fulfil all my duties as I should like to, and then, being so overburdened with my work and extensive journeys abroad, I am afraid that it might cause only trouble both to the Conservatoire and myself.

Thanking you, dear Sir, for your kind offer,

I remain, Your devoted and obliged,

Antonín Dvořák.

Dvořák to JUDr. Josef Tragy (1830-1914), lawyer and secretary of the Union for the Advancement of Music in Bohemia which administered the Prague Conservatoire of Music and was preparing for the amalgamation of this institute with the Prague Organ School for the year 1889-1890. The resolution that Dvořák should be appointed teacher of composition was taken on Jan. 25th 1889. Dvořák, however, declined the offer and only complied with a second resolution of the Union taken in October 1890 (see 141).

134. SELF-DISPARAGEMENT

...There was a lively scene at Urbánek's shop when the question came up of Dvořák becoming a teacher at the Conservatoire. "Me a teacher? Get away with you! My duty is to write, do you understand and not to teach. I am too much of an old bear, and nobody will get me into doing that." Fortunately they did win him for that work and how mistaken had been his earlier view was proved by the young generation which was trained under his guidance.

Ladislav Dolanský (see 73): from the book "Musical Memoirs".—At Urbánek's: i. e. the music shop of Fr. A. Urbanek in Prague (see 50).

135. DVOŘÁK'S SYMPHONY IN HAMBURG

...Dvořák's Symphony was exceptionally successful, it was magnificently played—because also conducted, much better, more plastically and a coeur than in Berlin. It was the most successful concert, this fourth one...

Hans von Bülow (see 114) in Hamburg to H. Wolff in Berlin, 21. XI. 1889.— Bülow conducted Dvořák's D minor Symphony, op. 70, the composer being present, on the 27th and 28th Oct. 1889 in Berlin and shortly afterwards in Hamburg (see 115).— H. Wolff see 131.

136. DVOŘÁK IN MOSCOW AND PETROGRAD

Dear Friend,   Petrograd, Sunday morning.

I promised that I would write to you and I am doing so now. Before you get this letter you will perhaps know from the papers how it fell out in Moscow—in my view well but not so well as I expected.

... That does not matter, however, for I still won a great moral victory in Moscow, at least so I was told in musical circles and the orchestra was greatly taken with my compositions and played with real enthusiasm.

The German "Gesangverein" is giving Stabat Mater today in Moscow, and at the church they showed me great attention. I was at the rehearsal and everybody was deeply affected and they gave me a laurel wreath. The director of the Society here is a certain Bartz, my ardent admirer. He wrote, too, about the concert to the Národní Listy and sent the same notice to the Neue Freie Presse and Politik. At a banquet at the "Slav Bazaar", he had a moving speech and sang my praises.

In Petrograd, on the other hand, my concert yesterday in the "Dvorjanskoe sobranie" turned out splendidly for me. The public and the orchestra gave me a very hearty reception and after each movement of the Symphony—it was the First in D major, there was great applause and after the Capriccio I had to bow repeatedly. At the Evropa Hotel, Rubinstein (President of the Russian Musical Society) gave a banquet in my honour. It was short but all the heartier. Rubinstein toasted me, Auer, the violinist, drank to the new Doctor of Music (all the papers had a telegram from Prague and so I was pleasantly surprised to learn of it here) I then drank a health to Rubinstein, whereupon the most outstanding musical critic and scholar (they call him "the Russian Hanzlík"), Laroche, toasted me most elegantly and said that the Czechs, though a small nation, stand high in science and art and wished that young Russia would follow our example. He writes for the Moscow papers and the literary papers here etc. The papers (Petersburg Gazette) brought a notice previous to the concert as did also the Deutsche Moskauer Zeitung about Stabat Mater and I send you the programme from here.

I am leaving this afternoon for Prague.

Your ever grateful

Antonín Dvořák.

13. Dvořák and his wife in London.

14. Dvořák's summer retreat in Vysoká.

Dvořák to his friend, Gustav Eim in Vienna, 23. III. 1890.—Eim (1849-1897) was a Czech deputy in the former Austrian Reichsrat in Vienna and the Vienna correspondent of the Prague daily, Národní listy.—For Dvořák's invitation to Russia see 130.— In Moscow Dvořák played, in addition to the Symphony mentioned, the I. Slavonic Rhapsody, the Scherzo capriccioso, the Symphonic Variations and the Adagio from the Serenade for Wind Instruments.—Stabat Mater was performed by the Deutscher Musikverein in Moscow on the 23rd March in the Church of St. Peter and St. Paul after Dvořák had left for Petrograd.—*Johannes Bartz* (1848-1933), composer, organist and choir-master in Moscow.—The celebrated Russian composer, *Anton Rubinstein* (1829-1894), was at this time director, for the last year, of the Petrograd Conservatoire and President of the Russian Musical Society.—*Leopold Auer* (1845-1930), a Hungarian violinist, from 1868 teacher at the Conservatoire in Petrograd.—*Herman A. Laroche* (1845-1904), a distinguished Russian music critic and writer, an intimate friend of Tchaikovsky.— "The new Doctor of Music": in March 1890 the Academic Senate of the Charles University in Prague awarded Dvořák the honorary degree of Doctor of Philosophy.

137. DVOŘÁK ON SMETANA

...Dvořák was very modest. I never heard him glorify himself at the expense of another composer, or speak of any with contempt. On the contrary, in every one, even the least significant, he found some qualities which he liked...

In 1893 when Smetana's Symphony was being rehearsed for the XXV. Popular Concert, Dvořák suddenly came in to see Velebín Urbánek and said in my hearing: "I have just been at a rehearsal of Smetana's Symphony. Man alive, that's a Scherzo! I'll never write anything like that if I live to be a hundred."

From "Musical Memoirs" by L. Dolanský (see 73).—Bedřich Smetana wrote his "Triumphal Symphony" in E major to which reference is here made, in 1853.

138. DVOŘÁK'S REQUIEM

Dear Friend,   Vysoká, 18 12/8 90.

You must know how it has long been my wish to see you here with us at Vysoká, and it is a pity that as yet it has not been possible—I hope, however, that you will be able somehow to manage to come to us this year if only for a short time, perhaps some Sunday or holiday.

I have finished the Requiem and now am scoring it and should be very glad to hear your sincere opinion of it. I am very hopeful and think, but I know it is so for certain, that I have succeeded in making another *step* or *more* forward, as compared with, for instance, Stabat Mater or my other larger works.

So I invite you once more to come if you possibly can and thereby give great pleasure to

Your sincerely devoted friend,

Antonín Dvořák.

Dvořák to his friend Emanuel Chvála (see 71).—Dvořák worked at his *Requiem* for solo voices, choir and archestra, op. 89, from the 1st January to the 31st October 1890.

139. VIENNA PERFORMANCE OF THE NEW SYMPHONY IN PROSPECT

Honoured Friend,   Prague, 18 16/10 90.

A thousand thanks for your kind and cordial letter which is once more for me an irrefutable proof of how, from the first days of our acquaintance, up to the present—and I hope for all days to come—you have vouchsafed me your dear friendship, for which I feel myself, honoured Friend and Patron, eternally indebted to you. May God reward you for it! — I have nothing, I cannot do anything—only my heart, my feelings say to me: "Keep to the path which leads us to the highest goal of noble art and therein will lie the greatest reward you can give!" And now to the matter in hand. I shall send you the score and parts a few days before the performance, which I regard as a high honour especially as being vouchsafed by you and your splendid Philharmonic. I thank you very, very much! — How I am looking for-

130

ward to it! For your kind invitation to your house accept my best thanks. So far so good—but will the success be accordingly? Do you believe in it? But your friendly letter, the delight which you have in the work augur well for its success and so I may hope that your art as a conductor will again, as so often in the past, bring me a happy day. With warmest greetings and kind regards to Madam, your wife,

I remain, Your ever grateful

Antonín Dvořák.

Dvořák to Richter in Vienna.—The letter refers to the new, now the eight Symphony in G major, op. 88, of which Dvořák prepared the sketch between the 6th and the 23rd of September and the score of which was completed by the 8th November 1889. Dvořák himself conducted the first performance of this work on the 2nd February 1890 with the orchestra of the National Theatre in Prague, and then on the 24th April of the same year with the Philharmonic Society in London. Richter intended to perform the Symphony with the Vienna Philharmonic on December 7th 1890, but, as a result of changes in the repertoire of the Hofoper, had to postpone it to January 4th 1891 (see 142) so that Dvořák was able to conduct the Symphony before then at the so-called Museum Concert in Frankfurt-on-Main (see 141).

140. ANOTHER POSTPONEMENT

15th November 1890.

Honoured Friend,

Your manuscript-score comes into my house and I shall guard it as the apple of my eye. The Symphony will be performed at the 3rd Concert, i. e. on the 7th December. Massenet is here with his new opera and so *I shall not have the necessary number of rehearsals* as "Cid" is also being studied for the first time. Truly disgusting!—Then I must have a number of new copies made of quartet parts. I wish to give your work a *perfect* performance and for that I need time; and I shall have time after the 2nd Concert. So — December 7th!

Yesterday at Hellmesberger's I heard your new piano quintet: really splendid. It gave me great pleasure and enjoyment. You will come in any case to the 2 last rehearsals. Everything is arranged and I hope that you will also be satisfied with the presentation of your lovely work. Please send a card saying *when* you will arrive in Vienna and at what station.

Your sincerely devoted

Hans Richter.

Richter to Dvořák in Prague.—See 139 and 142.—The very successful Piano Quintet in A major, op. 81 was composed between August 18th and October 3rd 1887 (see also 141).

141. APPOINTMENT TO THE PRAGUE CONSERVATOIRE AND FURTHER SUCCESSES

Dear Friend,   Prague, 18 17/11 90.

I have a lot to tell you, in the meantime only the most interesting items, so listen! I have accepted the professorship at the Conservatoire (composition and instrumentation) and received a flattering letter from Prince Ferdinand of Lobkowitz in which he informed me that my appointment was received with great satisfaction and unanimously.

Then I was in Frankfurt and conducted my new Symphony and the "Hussite" with great success. It was wonderful! I wish you could have heard the orchestra! 20 first violins, 20 seconds, 16 violas, 14 cellos and 12 doublebasses. Some papers wrote against but others enthusiastically for my composition, perhaps you have read them in the Politika? I have just received a letter from Richter in which he tells me that they will give my new Symphony on December 7th and that at the request of the Philharmonic and of Richter himself I must go to Vienna for it. In short he writes to me about the Symphony in enthusiastic terms and thinks that I shall be very pleased with the performance. Of that I have certainly no doubt.

Then in Vienna last week they played (Hellmesberger) my Piano Quintet which was also very well received. I am curious what the papers will write *now* and especially Hanslik. The work is being given everywhere in Germany and is greatly liked, they say it will be *popular*. So you see how I am getting on.

Also my new piano quartet in E flat major is being played in Munich and Frankfurt and is a great success.

And now I have just got a letter from England saying that the University of Cambridge wishes to honour me by conferring on me the degree of Doctor "honoris causa". What do you say to that? I must go there, however, and receive the degree in person. It is an elaborate ceremony and then I must conduct Stabat Mater and one of my symphonies. It is, so I am told, a rare distinction and the only foreign artist who has it is Joachim. Of course it goes without saying that I shall accept it. The Requiem is, thank goodness, finished, but if I give it to Novello, Simrock will, so he says, take the matter to court. He wishes to sue me but I am not afraid. Of this another time. I must finish as I have no more room.

Your affectionate friend,

Ant. Dvořák.

Dvořák to A. Göbl (see 33) at Sychrov.—The choral and musical society "Žerotín" in Olomouc celebrated its tenth anniversary on the 15th and 16th November 1890. At the second concert, the honorary members of the society, Dvořák, Fibich and Bendl conducted their own works.—Dvořák was, after all, appointed teacher of composition at the Conservatoire in Prague on condition that he take up his duties as from January 1st 1891 and that he teach 7-8 months in the year. Prince Ferdinand Lobkowitz being President of the Union for the Advancement of Music in Bohemia, which administered the Conservatoire.—At the Museum Concert in Frankfurt-on-Main, Dvořák conducted the G major Symphony and the Hussite Overture (see 138).—For the intended performance of the Symphony in Vienna and the performance there of the Piano Quintet in A major see 139. The *Piano Quartet in E flat major*, op. 87, was composed between the 26th August and the 8th November 1889.—Of the conferring of the honorary degree of Doctor of Music by the University of Cambridge, Dvořák was informed in a private letter from the English Anglo-Irish composer, *Charles V. Stanford* (1852-1894) who asked him to accept this distinction and at the same time informed him that he would have to be present at the "capping" ceremony.—The dispute regarding the publication of the Requiem ended with its publication by the firm of Novello in London.

142. MORE DELAYS IN VIENNA

Honoured Friend,

Would you do me a favour? I hope so.—The repertoire situation is so unfavourable that I cannot include in the programme of the next concert any new work. Would you be so good and friendly as to let me keep the loaned score and parts till the 5th Concert, that is till the 4th January? By that time all difficulties with the repertoire will be overcome (two new ballets and a Wagner cycle) and then I can apply myself properly con amore to the study of your splendid Symphony. I do not know any better new work with which I could open the first concert in the New Year. If it is possible I shall arrange for it to be put on at the beginning of the programme so that the last movement does not suffer by the noise of people leaving before the end. So I beg you to grant my request... At my house you will be comfortable also in the New Year. Asking you once again kindly to agree to my proposal.

I am, With warmest greetings,
Your sincerely devoted

Hans Richter.

Richter in Vienna to Dvořák in Prague, 29. XI. 1890.—Viz also 139.

143. DVOŘÁK REGRETS

Prague 18 1/1 91.

Honoured Friend,

I regret extremely that I cannot come to the performance as my *obligations* in connection with my new calling at the Prague Music Conservatoire are such that I cannot possibly absent myself at the very beginning of my activities.

It is very painful for me to have to deny myself the pleasure of hearing my work from you, but that is how the matter stands and there is nothing to be done. Thanking you warmly for the kindness you have so repeatedly shown me,

I remain, Ever gratefully yours,

Antonín Dvořák.

Dvořák to Richter in Vienna.—It is quite possible that the postponements in the performance of the G major Symphony had annoyed Dvořák and that it was for that reason that he did not go to Vienna on this occasion, to the great regret of Richter as is to be seen from the following letter.

144. RICHTER BOTH SORRY AND GLAD

Dear bad Friend,

You would certainly have been pleased with this perform-ance. All of us felt that here was a splendid work: and so we were all enthusiastic. Brahms dined with me after the perform-ance and we drank to the health of the unfortunately absent father of No. 4. Vivat sequens.

Your devoted

Hans Richter.

The success was warm and hearty.

Richter to Dvořák in Prague 5. I. 1891.—The father of no. 4: the Symphony was designated as the fourth in the order of publication, though it was actually the eigth in the order of composition.

145. DVOŘÁK AT THE CONSERVATOIRE

...The day will never fade from my memory on which I handed over to him the school of composition. It took place on a special Composition Evening, on the 14th January 1891, in the

135

small concert hall of the Conservatoire, a moment of undoubted historic importance when, for the first time in the eighty years of its existence, the institute presented to the public its own school of composition. Dvořák was unusually moved by the compositions performed and declared that the results far exceeded his expectations. The next day those pupils who had been assigned to Dvořák (I chose out of the whole number the 12 most talented) took leave of me; I kept the rest myself to the end of the year. And in the same measure as he had been at first unwilling to accept the post and did so only at the insistent persuasion of the above-mentioned office-holders, so now teaching at school became for Dvořák a necessity that he looked forward to daily. Originally he was to teach an hour every day (from 8–9 a. m.); but his lesson not seldom went on the whole forenoon, which upset the rest of our time-table. In the following year the pupils were divided into three groups with two hours a week, or 2 groups with three hours a week.

...Of the pupils he had in the first year of his teaching, the most outstanding were Josef Suk (later his son-in-law) and Oskar Nedbal. The next year they were joined by Vítězslav Novák. And then there passed through his hands innumerable pupils of different degrees of talent, maturity and perseverence. As to the compositions which arose during, I think, Dvořák's second year of teaching, a specially noteworthy curiosity was a symphonietta for small orchestra, an extremely interesting composition worked out on the blackboard at school and publicly performed at the Final Examination of the Conservatoire, which was the common spiritual product of 12 pupils.

From the reminiscences of *Karel Stecker* (1861-1918), composer and professor of composition at the Prague Conservatoire.—Dvořák was appointed professor of instrumentation, the elements of form and practical instruction in composition, and entrusted with the training of the third year students with the proviso that he would be assigned only specially talented students.

146. STUDENT RECOLLECTIONS: VÍTĚZSLAV NOVÁK

What kind of a teacher was Dvořák? The answer can be given in two words: a teacher-artist. He was a teacher only for the talented. Pupils who got to him through inadvertance or out of curiosity he managed to get rid of very quickly. "Music is a liberal art," he would often say on such occasions. He was remarkably practical, submitting each work to a detailed examination, drawing attention to our awkward places and mistakes in very apt comments. "Sometimes I could howl, but we learn a lot from it", Josef Suk once sighed. And he was absolutely right. Dvořák's school was strict but as salutary as a cold douche. Dvořák, however, was never pedantic and praised an original idea with undisguised pleasure...

From the funeral oration at Dvořák's grave.—Vítězslav Novák (1870-1949), along with Josef Suk the most outstanding student of Dvořák's school of composition and a leading representative of modern Czech music.

147. STUDENT RECOLLECTIONS: JOSEF MICHL

And so only slowly, often at the cost of bitter experience, did we get to know the Master and grasp his principles and requirements. Unfortunately not even then did we succeed in satisfying our strict Master in every respect. Dvořák had his moods and like every great spirit, he, too, suffered from so-called "Divine discontent". So, for instance, he would like certain parts in our compositions and on first seeing them he might be even positively enthusiastic; later, however, he no longer liked the same parts and required us to change them, improve them or even replace them with better passages. As a result, many compositions or little pieces which were thought to be definitely finished had to be gone over again and sometimes practically re-composed. It can easily be imagined that such work was not as a rule easy, the less so as the Master did not usually indicate how the correction was to be carried out—*and himself only very rarely made the correction. And here we strike on the most typical feature of his method: if he found something* (and that happened very often) *with which he did not agree and which he wanted to have differently and better written, he forced us to think about it and did not give in till we had found a better way.* It caused us not a few very unpleasant moments and a lot of difficulty, but to be quite sincere, it was for us a real blessing: "What good would it be to you," he would often say, "if I were to write it the way it should be! It wouldn't be yours then and every musician worth his salt would know that somebody had put it right for you. Anybody who wants to compose must get accustomed to think and work independently!"

From the study *"A Year under Dvořák".*—Josef Michl (see 4).

148. STUDENT RECOLLECTIONS: JOSEF SUK

Dvořák's knowledge of musical works was truly astounding. Bach, Handel, Gluck, Haydn, Mozart, Beethoven, Schubert, Berlioz, Wagner, Liszt,—he knew the works of all these masters in detail. He did not dislike Italian music nor did he share the view of the time that it was "hurdy-gurdy". And, in general, there was no movement of which he did not take notice; he studied Bruckner, was interested in Richard Strauss and was pleased when he saw among his students a striving after new and independent expression. I brought to one of our first lessons a trio, a little composition from my boyhood days. On going through the second movement, which had a Dvořák colouring, he gave me a friendly look and remarked: "I have heard something like it; seek and seek again, young man, as we had to seek." He was interested in everything, nothing in our lives escaped his attention. He liked to read the papers and critical notices, both home and foreign, and read regularly Czech provincial papers, for he took a lively concern in the cultural activities of the countryside.

From the article: "Some Reminiscences."—Josef Suk (see 1).

149. STUDENT RECOLLECTIONS: VÍTĚZSLAV NOVÁK

What was his relation to the giants of music? He paid homage to Beethoven whom he continually held up to us as an example; he admired Wagner and Berlioz, he valued Brahms greatly and loved Schubert with whom he was spiritually akin. This list of names, though incomplete, shows that Dvořák's taste was by no means one-sided. The Master was acquainted with all of beauty and originality that had been created in music and his comments and comparisons were always interesting and often very original...

See 146.

150. DVOŘÁK ON MOZART

...Another time he surprised us with the question: who of us knows *what Mozart is?* The mysterious question caused much cudgelling of brains and many views were put forward about Mozart's significance. They were, however, only the usual commonplace phrases such as: Mozart is a classic—a composer of opera–of symphonies–Haydn's successor–Beethoven's antipode–a precursor of Romanticism and similar more or less senseless sentences. To all the answers the Master shook his head and the enigma remained unsolved.

"Now that just shows how little sense and feeling you have for music. Do you mean to say that not one of you can guess?!"–he asked, raising his voice.

Nobody replied. ...Dvořák's temperament boiled over: Seizing the nearest pupil by the shoulder, he dragged him to the window and here–pointing with one hand to the sky and with the other shaking the pupil by the sleeve–asked him once more: "Now do you know? *Do you see it?*"

– – –The pupil was in obvious embarrassment: now throwing an inquiring look at the Master, now gazing at the sky, he finally stuttered:

"Excuse me, sir, I don't see anything."

"What? You don't see the sun?"

"I see it!"

"Why then don't you say what *Mozart* is?"

And turning away from the window–seriously, loftily and with tremendous enthusiasm, Dvořák pronounced this significant sentence:

"Well, remember: *Mozart is sunshine!*"

From the article: "From Dvořák's School" by Josef Michl (see 4).

151. DVOŘÁK–RAPHAEL–MOZART

...When we were in London (or shortly before), the London National Gallery had enriched its collections with the purchase at great cost of a Madonna by Raphael. Dvořák knew the Gallery from his earlier visits, but we went in again together. Before the Madonna, which he had not seen as yet, Dvořák stood long in silence. At last he began: "You see, that is Mozart. It is so beautifully composed. The landscape behind the throne, you do not know why it is there, but it is lovely and must be like that. In Brussels they have pictures by Breughel, tremendous pictures,"—it was not till years later in Brussels that I realized that the word "tremendous" referred to the content of the pictures and not to their size—"they positively overpower you and you realize how small you are.—And that is Beethoven." How Dvořák loved Beethoven I do not need to tell you; but Mozart had no less firm a hold on his affection. Dvořák was heart and soul an artist to whom art of all styles appealed—even though he had his own style—if only it was truly beautiful. I shall never forget, for instance, what heavenly bliss illumined his countenance when we were listening to Mozart's D minor Concerto at a Popular Concert at the Crystal Palace near Sydenham. Or what sacrilege it seemed to him when (and as was his habit he did not hesitate to express himself very clearly) one of our composers complained how little recognition he had won so far and what success Mozart achieved in his early years.

From the article: "With Dvořák in London" by J. Zubatý (see 8), who accompanied Dvořák to England on his third visit in 1885.

152. DVOŘÁK AT CAMBRIDGE

Cambridge,

Dear Friend,   (forenoon) 16th June 1891.

Today, Tuesday, at 12 o'clock, I shall be a Doctor. Besides me there will be about six others, a Russian etc., and then the British Ambassador to Rome has also arrived. Yesterday's concert turned out splendidly as usual.—The lovely doctor's cap and gown were gifted to me by the University. I shall tell you all about the rest later.

God bless you! Yours,

A. Dvořák.

Dvořák to A. Göbl at Sychrov.—On the evening before the graduation, an official concert was held in the University town of Cambridge on June 15th 1891, at which Dvořák, in place of a dissertation, conducted his G major Symphony and Stabat Mater. Along with Dvořák, degrees were conferred on Mechnikov, the Russian zoologist, and several English scientists.

153. AT THE GRADUATION CEREMONY

...A delightfully pawky sense of humour characterizes a reference to the Master's graduation in Cambridge. At school they were talking about some celebration which provoked the Master to the following comment: "I don't like such celebrations. And if it so happens that I must be present at one I am (as it were) on pins and needles. I shall never forget how I felt when they made me a doctor in England: the formalities and the doctors. All the faces so grave and it seemed that none could speak anything but Latin. I listened to my right and to my left and did not know where to turn my ear. And when I discovered that they were talking to me I could have wished myself anywhere else than there and was ashamed that I did not know Latin. But when I look back on it today I must smile and think to myself that to compose Stabat Mater is, after all, better than to know Latin."

From Reminiscences by Josef Michl (see 4).—The Dean of the Faculty introduced Dvořák in a Latin ovation in which he brought out the significance of Dvořák as a composer with special emphasis on Dvořák's works then being performed in England.

154. AN INVITATION TO AMERICA

Dear Friend,   18 20/6 91.

Yesterday, after 40 hours of travelling, we arrived home safely. Everything turned out splendidly—as I already informed you in my letter from Cambridge. It will remain an unforgettable memory for the rest of my life. It would take me a long, long time to tell you about it. Perhaps you will read of it in the papers. Novotný is with me just now and making notes of everything.

I am to go to America for 2 years.

The directorship of the Conservatoire and to conduct 10 concerts (of my own compositions) for 8 months and 4 months vacation, for a yearly salary of 15,000 dollars or over 30,000 gold francs. Should I take it? Or should I not? Write me a word or two. I am waiting for *Dr. Tragy* before I make a decision. Write to me at Vysoká which I am leaving for *tomorrow*, Monday, with my family.

With affectionate greetings to Yourself and kind regards to all at Sychrov,

Yours,

A. Dvořák.

Dvořák to A. Göbl at Sychrov.—To invite Dvořák to be the Director of the National Conservatory of Music of America in New York was the idea of the founder and President of this institute, *Mrs. Jeanette M. Thurber* (1852—1946). Dvořák received the first call from her in the form of a telegram from Paris on June 6th 1891, where she was staying at the time.—Novotný see 2, Dr. Tragy see 133.

155. DVOŘÁK CONSIDERS THE AMERICAN OFFER

Vysoká, 18 1/8 91.

Dear Friend,

You are no doubt wondering why I haven't written to you for so long. I want to get the most out of this short stay in Vysoká and so I decided—to let my pen rest a while. I walk the whole day in my garden and amuse myself with my pigeons. That is my occupation here. But that will not interest you greatly. And so I must tell you that I have done something after all—I have finished the new "Overture" which I began in Prague. What name it will go by I do not know yet—but I read in the newspapers that it will be called "A Summer Night". People catch at whatever they can hear and parrot it after me—and all the time they don't really know anything.

And now something about America. Yesterday I got a copy of the contract. It is very long but I don't know yet whether I shall accept it. It seems that I should have 3 hours a day teaching composition and instrumentation and, in addition, prepare in 8 months 4 concerts with the pupils of the Conservatory and give 6 concerts in American towns at which the main works to be performed would be Stabat, The Spectre's Bride, Ludmilla, Requiem, Symphonies and Overtures etc. For that I should get 15,000 dollars or, in Czech money, 35,000 gulden. Before I leave they will deposit half the remuneration in Prague and the other half I should get by the month in advance. There is only one little hitch. I want the 7,500 dollars to be paid up by the end of *May* 1893 so that I could have holidays in June, July, August and the first half of September — which I should prefer to spend in Bohemia. If they meet this condition I shall probably accept. What people say of America is very mixed. As always in this world some are for and some against. Whether I shall get to see you or not I cannot say. In any case I should pay you a visit in October on my return from England. Then we shall have a lot to talk about. Especially about the Requiem and how it turned out in Birmingham. Very soon I shall be getting the arrangement for piano and I shall send you a copy at once.

We all send our affectionate greetings and especially

Your

A. Dvořák.

Dvořák to A. Göbl at Sychrov.—The new Overture: *"In Nature's Realm"*, op. 91, the first part of the trilogy: *"Nature, Life and Love"*, of which the other parts are the overtures *"Carnival"* op. 92 and *"Othello"*, op. 93. Dvořák worked at these composition from March 31st to January 18th 1892. On the sketch for the first overture is writen "Ouvertura lyrica" or "In Nature's Realm" or "A Summer Night". All three overtures are connected by the basic theme of Nature as the giver of all life, beauty, joy (Carnival) and sorrow (Othello, partly based on Shakespeare's drama).—The Requiem was first performed under Dvořák's baton at the Musical Festival in Birmingham on October 9th 1891. It was Dvořák's eighth visit to England (see also 138).

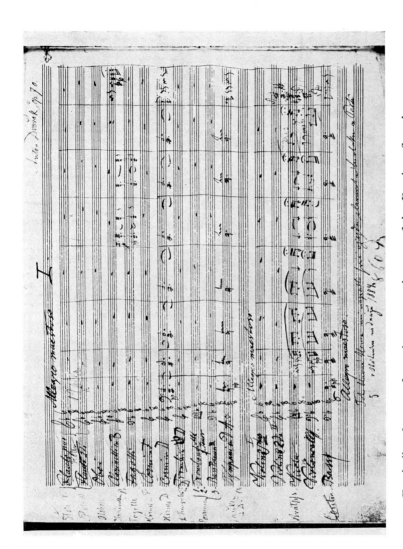

15. Facsimile of a page from the autograph score of the D minor Symphony, op. 70.

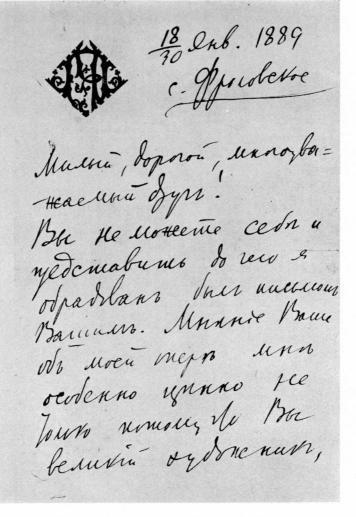

16. Facsimile of a page of a letter from P. I. Tchaikovsky.

156. NEGOTIATIONS WITH AMERICA

Dear Friend,   Prague, 24. 10. 91.

Thank you first of all for having sent what I asked for my pigeons. They will have a fine feed!

You will probably have read that I am safely back from England and that the Requiem was a tremendous success.

...Yesterday I sent the contract, revised for the third time, to London, and if they agree to all my changes—I shall sign. In America they write a great deal about my coming and have great expectations of my artistic activity.

Well, there will be a fine to-do when I get there! And then the Czechoslovaks – how they are looking forward, as I hear, to my arrival!

Once more my warmest thanks,
                        Your affectionate friend,
                                    Antonín Dvořák.

Dvořák to Aug. Bohdanecký in Čimelice.—Bohdanecký, Rus's son-in-law, was manager of an estate in the neighbouring village and often supplied Dvořák's garden at Vysoká with cuttings.

157. ON THE EVE OF DEPARTURE

Dear Friend,

I should have written to you long since, but in the last few days I have had, especially at the Academy, a number of strenuous (at least for me) sessions so that I am rather late in replying and beg you to kindly forgive my remissness...

I am well, thank God, and am now working at my III. Overture, Nature, Life and Love, but I still have a great piece of work ahead of me. I think that probably in Lent, when they will be giving my Requiem at the theatre, I shall present this novelty and it will be at the Conservatoire concerts. How happy I should be to see you there—but no hope of that!

Simrock has remembered my existence, he was probably sorry at not having heard anything about me for so long. He would like to have something again but I am letting him wait in the meantime to punish him. If he doesn't pay me very well, I shan't give him either the "Overtures" or the "Dumky". I shall always be able to get them accepted. I won't allow myself to be done down by him any more! — — —

Today Velebín Urbánek came to see me in connection with arrangements for my concerts with my pupils. They will be held in Bohemia and Moravia and everywhere we shall play the "Dumky" and some chamber music, and as Mladá Boleslav and Turnov will probably be included in the tour, I am hoping and looking forward to seeing you for certain in Turnov.

And now au revoir!

Your loving friend,

Antonín Dvořák.

Dvořák to A. Göbl at Sychrov, 25. XI. 1891.—Dvořák was one of the first members of the Czech Academy of Sciences and Arts.—III. Overture: "Othello" see 155.—The Requiem was first performed in Prague on the 25th April 1892 at the National Theatre. Dvořák presented the three overtures, op. 91-93, for the first time in Prague at a special farewell concert held on April 28th 1892 before his departure for America.—

Velebín Urbánek (see 50) arranged a number of "farewell" concerts in Czech and Moravian towns in the first five months of 1892. At these concerts, members of the teaching staff of the Prague Conservatoire, the violinist *Ferdinand Lachner* (1856-1910) and the violincellist *Hanuš Wihan* (1855-1920), later a member of the famous Bohemian Quartet, also played with Dvořák his new chamber work: the "Dumky" piano trio, op. 90, composed between November 1890, and the 12th February 1891. ("Dumka" is the name of a Ukrainian folk-song — half melancholy, half wildly gay.)

158. AMERICAN JOURNEY

...I made Master Dvořák's acquaintance during my studies at the Prague Conservatoire to which I came from my native town of Spillville and where I finished in 1892...

When, on taking my final examinations at the Conservatoire, I mentioned that I would be leaving as soon as possible for America, the Master said quite simply: "You know what—we shall do it like this: you will wait till September and then we shall go nicely together." On my asking what I should do in Bohemia for two whole months, the Master said: "You will come for the holidays to our place at Vysoká and then we shall set out together for America!" And that was what happened.

At Vysoká life ran in the channels cut out by the Master during his previous visits. The Master himself was very diligent this summer. First of all he finished the "Te Deum" which was to be given its first performance at his first appearance in New York and then, when an English poem reached him from Mrs. Jeanette M. Thurber, the founder of the National Conservatory in New York, he started work on the cantata "The American Flag", the sketch for which he had completed before his departure for America. Otherwise the quiet tenor of life at Vysoká was considerably enlivened by the arrival on a visit of Oskar Nedbal and Josef Suk who were to work out the piano arrangement of some of the Master's works. Especially Nedbal was up to all sorts of pranks which sometimes made the Master really angry...

In the middle of September 1892, the Master, with his wife, his daughter Otilie and his son Antonín, set out on the journey to America. We left Prague at 3 o'clock in the afternoon—on a Thursday—: at the station a lot of the Master's friends had come to see him off, and the last word the Master addressed to them was "au revoir in summer!" On Friday we were in Bremen and on Saturday we boarded the s. s. *Saale*, which was to convey us across the ocean. The ship weighed anchor at about 1 p. m., and at 5 p. m. on Sunday we reached Southampton in England from where the Master sent a telegram to the children who had remained behind in Prague that "everything is all right, all well".

The voyage lasted nine days and was very pleasant on the

whole, except for three days when it was quite stormy and all the passengers, with the exception of the Master, kept to their cabins. The Master proved an excellent sailor; the whole day, it might be as stormy as you like, he walked up and down the deck. Several times it happened that he was the only one to put in an appearance in the dining-room, and when Capt. Rinck saw him so alone, he invited him to his table. When they had breakfasted or dined at their ease, they lit their cigars and chatted.

On Monday, the 26th September, if I am not mistaken, after 6 o'clock in the evening, the ship docked in New York harbour. Here the Master was met by Mr. Santon, then Secretary to the National Conservatory, who, after the usual customs examination, took us to the Clarendon Hotel where a room had been reserved for the Master—complete with concert grand. The Master did not, however, find it quiet enough there and longed for a private lodging. This was found, at last, in no. 327 East 17th Street, opposite the Stuyvesant Park—with a Mrs Drew— and as the Conservatory was in the same street, nos. 128-130, the Master had not far to go.

From *Josef Jan Kovařík's Reminiscences.—Kovařík*, a native of Spillville, Iowa (1870-1951), studied violin in the years 1888-1892 at the Prague Conservatoire. After his return to America, Dvořák procured for him the post of teacher of violin at the National Conservatory of Music of America, and for the whole three years of the Master's stay in America (1892-1895) lived with Dvořák as a member of the family. He adored Dvořák and was an invaluable and unselfish companion to him throughout his stay. This extract is taken from his *Reminiscences*. The cantata *"Te Deum"*, for solo voices, choir and orchestra, op. 103, and *"The American Flag"*, to words by the American poet, Joseph Rodman Drake, op. 102, were written at Vysoká in the summer of 1892, before Dvořák's departure for America, for the celebration of the quatercentenary of the Discovery of America, planned for the autumn of that year.—Staying with the Dvořáks at Vysoká, were besides Kovařík, Josef Suk (see 1) and the later notable Czech conductor, *Oskar Nedbal* (1874-1930). Suk carried out the piano arrangement there of Dvořák's overtures "In Nature's Realm" and "Othello" and of the "Te Deum", while Nedbal did the piano arrangement of "Carnival".

159. NEW YORK – FIRST IMPRESSIONS

New York, Wednesday 7 a. m., 18 12/10 92.

Dear Friend,

I promised to write to you and am doing so now and very gladly because when I write to the old country (as they say here) or, what is the same, to every good friend,–being thus engaged with him–it seems to me as if I saw him here before me. And so it is today. I see you, as on a fine autumn morning, walking through the Kroměříž Park and looking sadly at the trees from which the leaves are falling one by one. But what help is there? Nature, too, needs her *diminuendo* and *morendo* so that she may come to life again and gather herself up for a great *crescendo*, achieving then her full strength and height in a mighty *ff*.– Where have I got to?–what am I telling you? I should be writing to you about our journey–about our crossing to America and perhaps about things concerning me personally?

Well, listen!

Our journey was lovely except for one day when everybody on board was sick except me–and so after only a short period of quarantine, we arrived safely in the promised land. The view from "Sandy Hook" (harbour town)–of New York with the magnificent Statue of Liberty (in whose head alone there is room for 60 persons and where banquets etc. are often held)– is most impressive! And then the amount of shippping from all parts of the world?! As I say amazing. On Tuesday the 27th we reached the town (Hoboken) where all ships dock, and there we were awaited by the Secretary to the National Conservatory, Mr. Santon–and what gave me special pleasure–by a Czech deputation. We exchanged greetings and a few words and then– a carriage was waiting for us and in a short time we were in New York, and are still in the same hotel. The city itself is magnificent, lovely buildings and beautiful streets and then, everywhere, the greatest cleanliness. It is dear here. Our gulden is like a dollar. At the hotel we pay 55 dollars a week for three rooms, of course in the most central part of the city, "Union Square". That does not matter, however, for we shall not spend more than 5000, and so, I am thankful to say, we shall be able to leave the rest untouched. On Sunday the 9th, there was a big Czech concert in my honour. There were 3000 people present in the hall—and there was no end to the cheering and clapping. There were speeches in Czech and English and I, poor creature, had to make a speech of thanks from the platform, holding a silver wreath in my hands. You can guess how I felt! Besides you will learn about in later from the newspapers. What the American papers write about me is simply terrible—they see in me, they say, the saviour of music and I don't know what else besides! All the scientific and political papers have been writing and are still writing about me.

I must finish as I have no more room. A hundred thousand affectionate greetings from

A. Dvořák.

1st concert at the "Music Hall", 21st October. *Te Deum, Three Overtures*. Please address your letter: A. D. National Conservatory of Music 126–128. 17th Street *New York, North America.*

Dvořák to Dr. Emil Kozánek in Kroměříž, Moravia.—Dr. Kozánek (1856-1927), lawyer and president of the musical society "Moravan" in Kroměříž. He was on terms of very warm friendship with Dvořák from the year 1873 and Dvořák was often his guest at Kroměříž.—For the first days, the Dvořáks, along with Kovařík, stayed at the Clarendon Hotel at the corner of East 18th Street and 4th Avenue near Union Square.— The Czech colony in New York held a concert of "welcome" with a programme of his compositions on the 9th October 1892 in the Central-Turnverein-Hall.—The American press gave Dvořák a truly impressive reception. The dailies and the revues published his biography along with a critical evaluation of his works and his position in contemporary music.—The Music Hall—the *Carnegie Hall* at the corner of Seventh Avenue and 57th Street. — Here Dvořák's first concert on American soil took place (21st October 1892) at which the Boston Symphony Orchestra performed the three overtures: "In Nature's Realm", "Carneval" and "Othello", under the composer's baton.

Parker House, Boston (Hotel)
27. XI. 1892.

Dear Sir, Esteemed Madam,

I have been wanting to write to you for a long time but have always put it off, waiting for a more suitable moment when I could tell you something of particular interest about America and especially about the musical conditions here. There is so much to tell and all so new and interesting that I cannot put it all down on paper and so I shall limit myself to the most important things.

The first and chief thing is that, thanks be to God, we are all well and liking it here very much. And why shouldn't we when it is so lovely and free here and one can live so much more peacefully—and that is what I need. I do not worry about anything and do my duty and it is all right. There are things here which one must admire and others which I would rather not see, but what can you do, everywhere there is something—in general, however, it is altogether different here, and, if America goes on like this, she will surpass all the others.

Just imagine how the Americans work in the interests of art and for the people! So, for instance, yesterday I came to Boston to conduct my obligatory concert (every thing connected with it being arranged by the highly esteemed President of our Conservatory, the tireless Mrs. Jeanette M. Thurber) at which the Requiem will be given with several hundred performers. The concert on December 1st will be for only the *wealthy and the intelligentzia*, but the preceding day my work will also be performed for poor workers who earn 18 dollars a week, the purpose being to give the poor and uneducated people the opportunity to hear the musical works of all times and all nations!! That's something, isn't it? I am looking forward to it like a child.

Today, Sunday, I have a rehearsal at three o'clock in the afternoon and wonder how it will come off. The orchestra here, which I heard in Brooklyn, is excellent, 100 musicians, mostly German as is also the conductor. His name is Nikisch and he comes from somewhere in Hungary. The orchestra was founded by a local millionaire, Colonel Higginson, who gave a big speech at my first concert (a thing unheard of here), spoke of my coming to America and the purpose to be served by my stay here. The Americans expect great things of me and the main thing is, so they say, to show them to the promised land and kingdom of a new and independent art, in short, to create a national music. If the small Czech nation can have such musicians, they say, why could not they, too, when their country and people is so immense.

Forgive me for lacking a little in modesty, but I am only telling you what the American papers are constantly writing.— It is certainly both a great and splendid task for me and I hope that with God's help I shall accomplish it. There is more than enough material here and plenty of talent. I have pupils from as far away as San Francisco. They are mostly poor people, but at our Institute teaching is free of charge, anybody who is really talented—pays no fees! I have only 8 pupils, but some of them very promising.

And then not less so are the entries for the competition for prizes offered by Mrs. Thurber. 1000 dollars for an opera, 1000 for an oratory, 1000 for a libretto, 500 for a symphony, and, for a cantata, a piano or a violin concerto, 300 dollars each.

A great deal of music has come in from all over America and I must go through it all. It does not take much work. I look at the first page and can tell straight away whether it is the work of a dilettante or an artist.

As regards operas, they are very poor and I don't know whether any will be awarded a prize. Besides myself there are other gentlemen on the jury—for each kind of composition five of us. The other kinds of composition such as symphonies, concertos, suites, serenades etc. interest me very much.—The composers are all much the same as at home—brought up in the

German School, but here and there another spirit, other thoughts, another colouring flashes forth, in short, something Indian (something à la Bret Harte). I am very curious how things will develop.

As regards my own work, this is my programme: On Mondays, Wednesdays and Fridays, from 9–11, I have composition; twice a week orchestra practice from 4–6 and the rest of my time is my own. You see that it is not a great deal and Mrs. Thurber is very "considerate" as she wrote to me in Europe that she would be.

She looks after the administrative side herself–has a secretary– also a founding member of the co-operative (very wealthy), a Mr. Stanton, an intimate friend of Mr. Cleveland, whereas Mrs. Thurber is a Republican–, but in matters of art they get on very well together and work for the good of our young and not yet fully developed institute. And so it is all right. The second secretary is Mrs MacDowel and she is mainly in charge of the correspondence.

And now something about our domestic affairs. We live in 17th street East, 327 (only 4 mins. from the school) and are very satisfied with the flat. Mr. Steinway sent me a piano immediately–a lovely one and, of course, free of charge, so that we have one nice piece of furniture in our sitting-room. Besides this we have 3 others rooms and a small room (furnished) and pay 80 dollars a month. A lot for us but the normal price here.

We have breakfast and supper at home and go to a boarding-house for dinner.

I must stop. My kind regards to yourself and your wife,
I remain, Gratefully Yours,

Antonín Dvořák.

My wife, who is with me, asks to be remembered to you.

Dvořák to Mr. and Mrs. Hlávka (see 111) *in Prague.*—The musical society "Cecilie" in Boston performed Dvořák's Requiem there on the 29th and 30th November 1892, with the composer conducting. In the years 1889-1893, the conductor of the Boston

Symphony Orchestra was the distinguished German conductor, *Arthur Nikisch* (1855-1922), who was fery fond of performing Dvořák's works.—*Colonel Thomas W. Higginson,* founder of the Boston Symphony Orchestra, addressed Dvořák in as peech following the performance of the American Hymn at his first concert on October 21st 1892 (see 159).—*Grover Cleveland,* 1884-1888, and 1892-1897, President of the USA.— After October 6th 1892, the Dvořáks and Kovařík rented a flat of five rooms in a private two-storeyed house, no. 327 in 17. Street East, opposite the Stuyvesant Park, where they lived for the whole three years of their stay in America.

161. DVOŘÁK'S RECREATIONS

... The Master lived in New York very quietly and, I believe, more free from care than in Prague. The first year, however, when he left his children behind in Prague (Anna, Magda, Otakar and Aloisie) and then the last (third) year when he came to America with only his wife and son, Otakar, he often longed for his children. But the second year, when he had his whole family round him, was, I am firmly convinced, the happiest year of his life.

The Master in general did not go out anywhere. He regularly attended the concerts of the New York Philharmonic (besides which he was only twice at the Metropolitan Opera during his whole stay in New York), twice in succession he went to hear the Kneisel Quartet and twice he was at a concert of the Boston Philharmonic which now as then comes to New York five times in the season and gives ten concerts.

The Master did not go out into society and, if he happened to be invited somewhere, he usually declined the invitation. In America, too, social life is not the same as in Europe. The American, engaged all day in business, likes to spend the evenings at home with his family.

What the Master missed in America were his pigeons and locomotives. He felt the want of these two "hobbies" very much, but here, too, he at length found a modest substitute. One day we went with the Master to the Central Park where there is a small Zoological Garden and buildings with different kinds of birds. And then we came to a huge aviary with about two hundred pigeons. It was a real surprise for the Master and his pleasure at seeing the pigeons was great and even though none of these pigeons could compare with his "pouters" and "fan-tails", we made the trip to Central Park at least once and often twice a week.

With locomotives it was a more difficult matter. In New York at that time, there was only one station—the others were across the river (the city of New York is situated on the island of Manhattan). At the main station they did not allow anybody on to the platform except the passengers and it was in vain that we begged the porter to let us look at the "American locomo-tive". We travelled by overhead tram to 155th. Street, a good hour from the Master's house, and there, on a bank, waited for the Chicago or Boston express to go by. Only it took up a lot of time, nearly the whole afternoon, as we always waited for a number of trains so that it would be worth the journey – and then the Master found a new hobby in steamships. For one thing the harbour was much nearer and then, on the day of departure, the public was allowed on board, an opportunity which the Master made full use of.

There was soon not a boat that we had not inspected from stem to stern. The Master always started a conversation with the ship's captain or with his assistants, and so, in a short time, we knew all the captains and mates by name. And when a ship was due to sail we went there and watched it from the shore till it was out of sight. If it happened that the Master remained a little longer than usual at the Conservatory or was engrossed in his work at home and so forgot about the departure of the boat and there was no longer time to go to the harbour, we went by overhead tram to Battery Park (the most southerly tip of the City) and from there followed the ship in her outward journey for as long as she remained in sight.

In the evening then, after a game of "darda", we discussed

with the Master how many knots the ship had probably made, where she might be etc. In the morning, the first Master's work was to take the "Herald" and read the "shipping news".

From *J. J. Kovařík's Reminiscences* (see 158).—The first season 1892-93, Dvořák was in New York only with his wife, his daughter Otilie and his son Antonín. The other four children did not arrive till May 31st 1893, accompanied by Mrs. Dvořák's eldest sister, Terezia Koutecká.—The *Kneisel Quartet* was composed of the leading musicians of the Boston Symphony Orchestra: Fr. Kneisel, O. Roth, L. Svecenski and A. Shroeder. —Dvořák was a great pigeon-fancier and bred rare varieties at his summer residence at Vysoká (see also 188); in addition he had a passion for locomotives. In Prague he used to go to different stations, usually on his early morning walks, and was well versed in what locomotive ran on which route and knew the locomotive-drivers personally.— "Darda" a card game. Dvořák was fond of playing it at home and even though he did not play for money, he often got very worked up about it.

162. NEWSPAPER GOSSIP AND HOLIDAY PLANS

New York
Wednesday morning, 7 a. m. 18 12/4 93.

My dear Friend Doctor Kozánek,

In order to satisfy you straight I shall tell you at once that I am as fit as a fiddle and in good heart and (except for some trifles) very well off. Boys in the street and the policemen—and drunken Irish women in the street, these are the things that annoy me, but one gets accustomed and *disaccustomed* to everything. But don't think that the "dis" refers to my friends at home (God bless them!) I think of you every day—but I say so only because it is an old saying, that is, only for the sake of saying something. It's true that with many people it often is so, but I shall not get used to the "*dis*" and as to the accustomed "*to*" I have a good disposition and am not afraid of anything, not even of the bad, spiteful critics in Vienna and here, too.

I have not met with opposition but the papers here are terribly fond of gossip which not even Cleveland escapes—and so they wrote a variety of things about me and it was all what they call: *sensational g ssip*, nothing more. Have you read, perhaps, in Národní Listy the tattle about Stabat Mater? It was given in Brooklyn and here in New York. I was to conduct it there but then I did not as our president (an excellent woman and my staunch supporter), did not wish me to conduct when Madam Juch was singing—there had been some disagreement between them which, however turned out unfavourably for Madam Juch, and this was the reason for the rage of some of the papers. The local Czech newspapers copied it and then the Národní Listy from them. That is what you may have read, but Mrs. Thurber is in the right. I am to go to Chicago, too, but I do not know what arrangements will be made. On the 15th and 16th April they are going to give a grand performance of the "Requiem", I was to conduct but shall not be able to do so. Last week, on the 6th April, they gave "The Spectre's Bride" here, and previous to that I conducted the "Hussite".

A small but good choir, the soloists good, with one exception, the orchestra weak for such a big hall—the "Carnegie Hall", and so the full effect was not always achieved. In autumn, however, we shall have a big concert and I shall be conducting and it will be different. Here, too, some of the critics are against me but the others are all good friends and write fairly and sometimes enthusiastically. I should like to have still more enemies than I have in Vienna, with the great exception of Dr. Hanslick. I have a good disposition, I can stand a lot and still be quite ready to forgive them. As far as this is concerned, you may be quite at rest. I sit firmly in the saddle and I like it here except, as I say, for some trifles.

My wish to return to Bohemia will not be realized this year, we have decided otherwise.

The children and my sister-in-law, Mrs. Koutecká, are coming here and will leave Prague on the 23rd May, on board the "Havel" from Bremen, so that, God grant, on the 31st May I shall look upon the faces of my dear and long-missed children.

Then we shall go straight to Chicago, have a look at the Exhibition, and then set out for *our summer Vysoká* in the State of Iowa, for the Czech village of Spillville where the teacher and the parish priest and everything is Czech and so I shall be among my own folks and am looking forward to it very much.

The teacher, Mr. Kovařík (from Písek and here 26 years), and the priest, Mr. Bílý, a very lively fellow, so they say (from Budějovice in Bohemia), will be the people with whom I shall be in closest contact. I shall have *pigeons* there and maybe we shall even play *"darda"*? How grand it will be. The priest has two pairs of ponies and we shall ride to Protivín, a little town near Spillville. Here in America there are *names of towns and villages of all nations under the sun!!*

The State of Iowa to which we are going is 1300 miles from New York but here such a distance is nothing. Thirty-six hours by express and we are there. It is farther than from where you are to London. Very soon we are going to see Buffalo, a town near *Niagara* and so we shall see the gigantic waterfalls. How I am looking forward to it. And now, what shall I write to you about?

I have not much work at school so that I have enough time for my own work and am now just finishing my E minor Symphony. I take great pleasure in it and it will differ very considerably from my others. Well, the *influence* of America must be felt by everyone who has any "nose" at all. Now I am negotiating with Novello (he has also his firm and agents here) and so my most recent compositions will be published at last.

They are: 1. Overture in F major ,1. Overture in A major, 3. Overture in F sharp major, 4. Dumky..., 5. Rondo for 'cello, 6. Te Deum, 7. The American Flag for choir and orchestra, 8. Symphony in E minor

I have no room left again. More another time.

With affectionate greetings to You and to All,

Ant. Dvořák.

Write soon!

Tomorrow the Hamburg boat *"Columbia"* is sailing so I hope you will get this letter sooner.

Dvořák to Dr. Emil Kozánek (see 159) *in Kroměřiž in Moravia.*—Dvořák was not present at the performance of the Requiem in Chicago.—The concert with the "Hussite", which Dvořák conducted, and with "The Spectre's Bride", performed by the Church Choral Society, was held in the Carnegie Hall on the 6th April 1893.—Spillville, a settlement at the north-west tip of the middle American State of Iowa where Josef J. Kovařík was born and where his father was teacher and choir director. The settlement was populated mainly by emigrants from Bohemia.—The famous E minor Symphony, called *"From the New World"* was composed between the 10th January and the 24th May 1893 in New York. As regards its musical content, it is for the most part the expression of the strongly agitating effect of life in the new enviroment, while the middle movement is, at the same time, influenced by the reading of Longfellow's "Hiawatha" and also by reminiscences of the homeland.—Except for the cantata *"The American Flag"* all the compositions mentioned in the letter were published by Simrock in Berlin in 1894.

163. JOURNEY FROM NEW YORK TO SPILLVILLE

On Saturday, June 3rd 1893–the third day after the children's arrival, we set out for Spillville in Iowa–for our holidays.

Our "caravan" or squad numbered ten persons–the Master with his wife, Mrs. Koutecká, six children, a maid (brought by Mrs. Koutecká from Bohemia) and myself. The journey from New York to Spillville (about 1320 English miles or 2112 km) took us by way of Philadelphia, Harrisburgh, the Alleghany Mountains to Pittsburgh and from there via Chicago to Spillville. The Master took an immense interest in everything on the journey. I had constantly to explain what country we were passing through etc. The journey passed pleasantly, everything went smoothly, the train was up to time and the Master's interest kept growing.

On Sunday at 11 o'clock, we reached Chicago where my brother met us. There we made a ten-hour stop, in the afternoon we drove through the town and at 9 o'clock in the evening we set out again for Spillville. On Monday at 8. a. m. we were in McGregor (Iowa) where the train stopped for an hour, had breakfast, watched the sweeping currents of the Mississippi– and left again at 9 for our destination. The Master, after a good breakfast, was in excellent spirits, everything interested him greatly and he was specially glad that in two hours he would at last leave the train and be at our journey's end–in the country– and before we realized it, we had reached Calmar–our last station (the railway does not go on to Spillville). In Calmar we were met by my father, the Rev. Tomáš Bílý, parish priest in Spillville and a native of Lužnice by Třeboň and the Rev. František Vrba, parish priest in American Protivín (Iowa)–I do not remember what part of Bohemia he comes from. After a short exchange of greetings, the Master and his family got into the carriage and we set out on the last stage of our journey to Spillville–about 8 km.

When the Master decided to spend his holiday in Spillville, I wrote to my Father to ask him whether there was not a little house to let. There was not, however, and so Father secured a lodging with a Mr. Schmidt (a German) consisting of eight rooms, and Father also saw to having it furnished so that on our arrival everything was in readiness–except a piano.

In our family, Mother was always the early bird and when, on the following morning, she caught sight of the Master at 5 o'clock in the morning walking up and down in front of the school, she got a great fright as she thought something unpleasant must have happened to them in the house. She ran out and began asking the Master what had happened (she did not know that the Master was also an early riser) whereupon the Master replied: "Nothing happened–and yet a great deal. Imagine, I was walking there in the wood along by the stream and after eight months I heard again the singing of birds! And here the birds are different from ours, they have much brighter colours and they sing differently, too. And now I am going to have breakfast and after breakfast I shall come again."

17. Dvořák in the robes of an honorary doctor
of Cambridge University.

18. Jeanette Thurber.

He went off but was soon back—we, lazy ones, were only getting up—and asked at what time was mass, that he would like to play the organ. Mass was at seven. Meantime the other members of the Master's family had appeared and we went to church. The Master at the organ began "God before Thy majesty"— and we started singing, but the old women looked up in surprise to the choir to see what was happening. They were not accustomed to be disturbed at "silent mass" by the organ and singing. And so the Master sat at the organ every day except the days he spent in Chicago, Omaha and St. Paul. The old women got used to the Master's "disturbing" them and began to sing, too, which pleased the Master very much; things progressed so far, indeed, that after mass some granny of grandad ventured to address him: "Mr. Dvořák, the singing was fine today", and "What will you be playing us tomorrow?"

The Master's day in Spillville was more or less as follows: He got up about four o'clock and went for a walk—to the stream or the river—and returned at five. After his walk he worked, at seven he was sitting at the organ in church, then he chatted a little, went home, worked again (in Spillville Dvořák wrote the F major string quartet and the E flat major string quintet) and then went for a walk. He usually went alone—here he had none of the nerve storms which he sometimes suffered from in Prague—and often nobody knew where he had gone. Almost every afternoon he spent in the company of some of the older settlers. He got them to tell him about their bitter and difficult beginnings in America: the old men told him how they went to help with the building of the railway—40 miles from Spillville—and how they went the long distance to work on foot, while their wives with the children toiled on the farms.

In Spillville the Master scarcely ever talked about music and I think that was one of the reasons he liked being there and why he felt so happy there.

From *J. J. Kovařík's Reminiscences*, see 158.—During his sojourn in Spillville, Dvořák composed in quick succession the *String Quartet in F major*, op. 96 (June 8th to 23rd) and the *String Quintet in E flat major* (two violas) op. 97 (June 26th to August 1st, 1893). Both works reflect the mood of happy contentment evoked by a holiday in the country among his countrymen and yet in a milieu breathing the exotic atmosphere of the American countryside.

164. PUBLISHING RELATIONS RESUMED

Spillville, U. S. A.
28. 7. 93.

Dear Simrock,

I am spending my 4 months' holiday here in Spillville, a completely Czech place in the State of Iowa, 1300 miles from New York, with my whole family, where I am very happy, and where I also got your letters. Dear Friend, I am composing now, thank goodness, only for my pleasure. I am fairly independent, have a salary of 15,000 dollars (or 60.000 M)—and so am able to devote my leisure to composing and am content. I am, therefore, in no hurry to publish my works. If you recollect your correspondence in Prague—two years ago, you will easily understand why I am holding off publishing my works. In the meantime their number has been added to (by fairly large works) and I shall tell you once more what I have. 3 Overtures for orchestra (new), Dumky (Trio for Violin, 'cello and piano), Rondo for 'cello (new), Symphony in E minor (new), String Quartet in F major (new) and I am now working at a String Quintet (two violas). Then I have an arrangement for 'cello solo, "Silent Woods", based on "From the Bohemian Forest", which should be welcomed by 'cellists. All these works you could have (with the exception of the not yet completed quintet) if we could agree on the fee. The Overtures (1, 2, 3) for M2000.—the Dumky M2000.—the E minor Symphony M2000.—the Rondo ('Cello solo) M500.—altogether M7,500.—The title, inside as well, to be in both German and Czech.

I am not asking any more than what you have always paid me. I am not going to New York till the 15th September when school-year begins and await your answer here. I am afraid, however, the distance being so great (a letter takes 16 days) that a long correspondence would drag the business out endlessly and make it impossible for the works to be ready by October or November. But you know better about these things than I do.

I gave the Overtures at my first concert here in New York (the E minor Symphony has not been performed yet) and I think they are my best orchestral works. You could print the "Dumky" first. Also the Rondo and the piece for 'cello ("Silent Woods"). And anyhow if we come to some conclusion you can do as you think best. I can send you the piano arrangement (duets) of the 3 Overtures at once and they could be ready by October. I have not done the arrangement for piano duets of the Dumky. I think it is very difficult to do. I have thought about it time and again but it always seemed to me an almost impossible task. That is why I have delayed doing it. I am not in the mood for it and nobody else could or would do it to my satisfaction. I have not so much time and so I shall perhaps get it done by one of my pupils in New York. Now I have all 6 children here and am content. Next year in June I intend to go to Europe.

Best greetings from me and my wife, Your

Antonín Dvořák.

For new compositions see also 162 and 163.

165. "CZECH DAY" AT THE CHICAGO EXHIBITION

18 17/8 93, Spillville Winnesheik Co
Iowa U. S. of America

Dear Friend,

We have just come back from Chicago where, as you probably know, the 12th August was "Czech Day" at the Exhibition and I hasten to write and tell you something about this great day.

On this day there was a great procession of all American Czechs at the Exhibition where a big concert was held and a big Sokol display. There were about 30,000 Czechs in the procession and the concert was in the big Festival Hall (orchestra 114 performers) and I conducted my own compositions and Mr. Hlaváč from Russia conducted the other works by Czech composers. The orchestra, as also the rendering, was splendid and the enthusiasm general. All the papers wrote enthusiastically as you will probably learn from your papers. The Exhibition itself is gigantic and to write of it would be a vain undertaking. It must be seen and seen very often, and still you do not really know anything, there is so much and everything so big truly "made in America". In spite of everything there will be a big deficit and many people here at the Exhibition are complaining and especially in Chicago business is suffering badly.

In September, about the 17th, we are leaving here for New York and will stop for a day or two again in Chicago, and on the 25th September I must be back at school. So if you write, write straight to New York, for it will be the first days of September before you get this letter and I am afraid your letter would no longer find us in Spillville. Except for the great heat, we have spent a very nice and pleasant holiday among Czechs and the children are already saying that they will miss it here.

That I have written a new E minor Symphony and that I have a new quartet for strings you probably already know, and I hope that during the coming season all my compositions will come out. At last Simrock has eaten humble pie and says that he will take all my works. I knew that he must come first to me and not I to him. So I have punished him after all with my waiting. It will be a whole pile of things when it is published. Three Overtures, Dumky, Rondo, "Silent Woods", Symphony, Quartet and Quintet, besides which I have still the "Te Deum" and "The American Flag" for choir and orchestra which Mr. Novello is interested in. But I do not know whether or when we shall come to terms.

With affectionate greetings to All,

Entirely yours, Antonín Dvořák.

Greetings to all our Písek acquaintance.

Dvořák to A. Rus in Písek, Bohemia.—In 1893 a World Exhibition was held in Chicago.—At the concert in the Festival Hall, Dvořák conducted with the Festival Orchestra, whose permanent conductor was *Theodor Thomas* (1835-1905), his Overture "My Home", the G major Symphony and three "Slavonic Dances" from, op. 72. Hlaváč from Russia: a native Czech, *Vojtěch I. Hlaváč* (1849-1911) spent his whole life as a conductor of various orchestras in Russia.—For Simrock approaching Dvořák again see 164.

166. DVOŘÁK VISITS OMAHA AND ST. PAUL

18 15/9 93. Spillville, Winnesheik Co., Iowa.

Dear Friend,

Your last letter dated the 26th August arrived safely and I was very happy to get it. Thank you. You wish to have a letter, too, from Spillville—and it's now or never as we are going tomorrow, Saturday, by way of Chicago and Niagara Falls, and then straight on to New York where I am to start work on the 21st September. The three months spent here in Spillville will remain a happy memory for the rest of our lives. We enjoyed being here and were very happy though we found the three months of heat rather trying. It was made up to us, however, by being among our own people, our Czech countrymen, and that gave us great joy. If it had not been for that, we should not have come here at all.

Spillville is a purely Czech settlement, founded by a certain "Bavarian", "German", "Spielmann", who christened the place Spillville. He died four years ago, and in the morning when I went to church, my way took me past his grave and strange thoughts always fill my mind at the sight of it as of the graves of many other Czech countrymen who sleep their last sleep here. These people came to this place about 40 years ago, mostly from the neighbourhood of Písek, Tábor and Budějovice. All the poorest of the poor, and after great hardships and struggle they are very well off here. I liked to go among the people and they, too, were all fond of me, and especially the grandmas and grandads were pleased when I played to them in church "God before Thy Majesty" and "A Thousand Times we greet Thee".

I became very good friends with Father Bílý, as were also our children—and often we went to visit Czech farmers 4–5 miles away. It is very strange here. Few people and a great deal of empty space. A farmer's nearest neighbour is often 4 miles off, especially in the *prairies* (I call them the Sahara) there are only endless acres of field and meadow and that is all you see. You don't meet a soul (here they only ride on horseback) and you are glad to see in the woods and meadows the huge herds of cattle which, summer and winter, are out at pasture in the broad fields. Men go to the woods and meadows where the cows graze to milk them. And so it is very "wild" here and sometimes very sad—sad to despair. But habit is everything. I should have to go on and on telling you things and you would hear many curious things about this America. And now about comething else. Not long ago we went on a trip to the State of Nebraska, to the town of Omaha, where there are also many Czechs. I went to visit Mr. Rosewater (Czech from Bukovany). He is a personal friend of Harrison's and Cleveland's and of many outstanding politicians. He has grown rich here and his magazine, the Omaha "Bee", is the most influential in the West and, in general, he is highly esteemed and respected. We stayed with him the three days of our stay there. In the evening Czechs came to play me a "Standerl" and when we were leaving, an American band came, too, and played a few pieces. As you can imagine, a banquet was not wanting and we were very jolly and the Czechs were tremendously happy and so was I. Omaha is 400 miles from our place and then we went to visit—guess who?—Father Rynd whom I met on Czech Day in Chicago—and do you know where? in the State of Minnesotta—in the town of St Paul, 400 miles from Nebraska—where there are also many Czechs. He is a Moravian from Kojetín and so maybe we shall travel together. I hope very much that I shall be able to pay a visit home to Bohemia, if my contract is prolonged—or if it isn't—I must see Bohemia, no matter what. I hear that the papers at home are writing as if I wished to stay here in America for good! Oh no, never! I am very well off here, God be praised, I am in good health and am working well and I know that, as for my new Symphony, the F major String Quartet and the Quintet (composed here in Spillville)—I should never have written these works "just so" if I hadn't seen America. You will hear later, after their performance in New York. Simrock wrote and bought *everything I have* and so I hope that by Spring you will have some news of them. The "Dumky", Overtures, Symphony, Quartet, Quintet, Rondo etc., while the "Te Deum" and "The American Flag" for choir and orchestra will probably be published *by Novello*.

With affectionate greetings, Yours,

Antonín Dvořák.

Dvořák to Dr. Kozánek (see 159) in Kroměříž.—Eduard Rosewater, factory owner and publisher of the daily, "The Omaha Bee".—Cleveland see 170, Benjamin Harrison, President of the USA, 1888-1892.—The cantata, "The American Flag", was published by the firm of G. Schirmer in New York in 1895.

167. BACK IN NEW YORK

On the journey from Spillville to New York, we made a stop at the Niagara Falls. When the Master saw this—one of the world's wonders, he stood silent for a full five minutes, his gaze fixed on the huge cataracts of water hurling themselves from a height of 165 feet—and finally exclaimed: My goodness, what a symphony in B minor that will be....

...In the afternoon the Master used to visit the (former) Fleishmann café at the corner of Broadway and 10th Street where he met Anton Seidl, the then conductor of the New York Philharmonic and, at the same time, conductor of German and mainly Wagner opera at the Metropolitan Opera. Seidl was an outstanding conductor, especially of Wagner—he had lived in close contact with that musical giant for some considerable time—and so the Master very often asked Seidl about Wagner— how he worked and so on. They had very interesting conversations and also discussions which not seldom became decidedly "heated"—but in the end everything always ended well—both it seems thought over their conversation and then when they met the next day, one or other admitted that he had been "partly" mistaken—and it was all right.

One day the Master asserted that the best of Wagner's operas was "Tannhäuser"—with this Seidl did not agree and it gave rise to a long debate which did not finish that day. As soon as they met the next day, however, Seidl began—"Well, I was thinking over our yesterday's discussion the whole evening, I considered it from every angle and I admit that you are right —from the point of view of opera Tannhäuser is the best.—But do you know Siegfried?" When the Master said that he had seen it only once, Seidl, promised to send tickets for the next performance at the Metropolitan when he would be conducting.

The tickets came for seats in a box in the so-called "Diamond Horseshoe", a row of boxes whose holders arrive at the performance at the last moment or usually even after it has begun, bedecked and overloaded with diamonds—all in evening dress. Of all this, however, we at this time knew nothing. The Master put on an ordinary dark suit, I chose from my modest wardrobe the darkest I had—but it was still pretty light. Whenever the Master was to go anywhere, he was always in a hurry to be there in time, and on this occasion he made more than usual haste.

The attendant looked at us in considerable surprise—perhaps because of our dress, perhaps because he was not accustomed to show people to their boxes half-an-hour before the beginning of the performance. The auditorium was still practically empty and the Master, having pulled out his watch and looked at it, said: "We've been in rather too great a hurry." Then we watched the stalls gradually filling up and that helped us to pass the time. Suddenly voices were to be heard in the neighbouring box—the Master looked round and immediately moved one seat back—I followed suit. The neighbours had come in evening dress and those who came after them the same. And so we finally reached the wall—each in a corner and waited for the lights to go down. At last the opera began. Round about ceaseless chatter. The Master "looked" at the talkers but it had no effect. So he paid no more heed to them and, although their talk was disturbing, listened attentively. After the first act we went home. Our attendant again looked at us curiously—perhaps thinking to himself: "Strange customers these—when others are only beginning to come, they go home."

At their usual meeting, Seidl asked the Master the next day what he thought of "Siegfried". The Master confessed straight away that he had gone home after the first act. The rendering, what he had heard of it, was excellent but that he had enough of that perpetual and constantly repeated rhythm

From J. J. Kovařík's Reminiscences (see 158).—From the period of Dvořák's sojourn in America, a few pages with sketches of motifs for a B minor Symphony have, indeed, been preserved. It is not known, however, if they are in any connection with Kovařík's report of the episode at the Niagara Falls.—*Anton Seidl* (1850-1898), born in Budapest, a distinguished German conductor, was active in New York from 1886-1898. Previous to that he collaborated as the friend of Richard Wagner in the preparation for the first performance of the tetralogy "Der Ring der Nibelungen" in Munich.

168. DVOŘÁK ON WAGNER

... From the conversation which followed, I saw that the Master was very interested in Nietzsche: He put one question after another which exhausted practically all I knew about the philosopher and a good third of his questions remained unanswered. Finally the conversation was concentrated on the essay "Nietzsche versus Wagner" and here Dvořák said: "I think nobody in the world has written anything like it *against* Wagner. Nietzsche must have had a great brain and in many respects he is right. But in some things he does him injustice and great injustice. You know you can talk a great deal about Wagner and you can criticize a great deal, too—but he is undefeatable. What Wagner did nobody did before him and nobody can take it from him. Music will go its way, will pass Wagner by, but Wagner will remain, just like the statue of that poet from whom they still learn at school today—Homer. And such a Homer is Wagner!"...

Josef Michl (see 4): "*Z Dvořákova vyprávění*".—*Friedrich Nietzsche* (1844-1900), was at first an enthusiastic admirer of the Bayreuth reformer and in his essays "Die Geburt der Tragödie aus dem Geiste der Musik" (1872), he saw in Wagner the fulfilment of his dreams of a tragedy growing out of Classical Greece and the cult of Dionysus and Apollo. This admiration was further intensified in "Richard Wagner in Bayreuth", written in 1876. "Der Fall Wagner" (1888) and "Nietzsche contra Wagner" (1889) to which Dvořák refers, mark, however, a complete reversal of Nietzsche's view and attack Wagner sharply for his pessimism and nihilism, for the pathos of his music and for his sympathy with the Middle Ages and Catholic mysticism.

169. SEIDL AND "THE NEW WORLD" SYMPHONY

One day at the café, Seidl said that he had heard that the Master has a *new symphony* and asked him for permission to perform it at one of the next concerts of the New York Philharmonic. The Master thought it over—but on taking leave he promised to give Seidl the Symphony to perform. That was in the middle of November 1893. The following day Seidl informed the Master that the symphony would be given at the concert to be held about the 15th December and that he should send him the score as soon as possible. The same evening, before I set out with the score, the Master wrote at the last minute on the title-page, "Z Nového světa" ("From the New World"). Till then there was only E minor Symphony no. 8. The title "From the New World" caused then and still causes today, at least here in America, much confusion and division of opinion. There were and are many people who thought and think that the title is to be understood as meaning the "American" symphony, i. e. a symphony with American music. Quite a wrong idea! This title means nothing more than "Impressions and Greetings from the New World"—as the Master himself more than once explained. And so when at length it was performed and when the Master read all sorts of views on it whether he had or had not created an "American" music, he smiled and said, "It seems that I have got them all confused" and added: "at home they will understand at once what I meant." I do not know, however, if he was not in part mistaken about those "at home"...

At the first performance of the symphony—on the 15th December 1893, in the Carnegie Hall—at the Friday afternoon concert which, in distinction from the evening concert, was called a "public rehearsal", Dvořák was not present. I went alone—the Master and his family heard the symphony at the Saturday evening concert.

From *J. J. Kovařik's Reminiscences* (see 158).—*The Symphony "From the New World"* (see 162) was performed for the first time by Seidl with the orchestra of the Philharmonic Society of New York at a "public rehearsal" on December 15th and then at a concert on December 16th in the Carnegie Hall (see 171 and 172).

126-128 East 17th Street,
New York.

The National
Conservatory of Music of America.
Office Hours, 9 To 12 and 2 To 4.

Dear Dr. Tragy,

I have not yet received any reply to my last from Spillville, Iowa, where I spent 4 months' holiday.

Now, however, I have something else that I must tell you. I am to prolong my contract for a year or two years and I wanted to ask your advice what I should do. My family circumstances require me to put aside enough to ensure a provision for my old age—you know very well that I love my country above all else and am glad to offer my humble services where they are needed and wanted, and that I wish, after my return to my country, to go on working for the good and development of our national art and shall, with God's help, fulfil what I have dedicated my life to and what I have dreamt of.

So, dear and esteemed Friend, if my *family* interest requires me to stay one or two years longer, be assured that at your call, should it be necessary—I shall gladly return to my country and beg you, if it is not troubling you too much, to send me your answer *straight away* so that I may inform Mrs. Thurber (our president) of my decision.

With the expression of my greatest respect,
I am, Yours truly,

Antonín Dvořák.

New York, 18 16/11 93.

My new E minor Symphony will be given here on the 15th and repeated on the 16th. It will be conducted by the well-known Wagner pupil, Anton Seidl, director of the Philharmonic Society of New York.

Dvořák to Dr. Josef Tragy (see 133) *in Prague.*—Dvořák held the appointment in New York for another two school-years, i. e. 1893-94 and 1894-95.

171. TRIUMPH OF THE NEW WORLD SYMPHONY

... The famous Czech composer would certainly not be easily satisfied if he were not extremely satisfied with the enthusiasm which his new symphony evoked in a very large audience. After the second movement he was given an enthusiastic ovation. Storms of applause resounded from all sides. Everyone present turned to look in the direction in which the conductor, Anton Seidl, was looking. It was clear whither their gaze was directed. At last a sturdily built man of medium height, straight as a fir-tree from the forest, whose music he so splendidly interprets, was discovered by the audience. From all over the hall there are cries of: "Dvorak! Dvorak! And while the composer is bowing we have the opportunity to observe this poet of tone who is able to move the heart of so great an audience. He has a dark complexion, dark hair, thin in front. His short, dark beard is beginning to turn grey. The large dark eyes are steady. His face is honest and friendly and its expression reveals an open and guileless nature. This is the man whom the audience is applauding. Dr. Dvořák, hands trembling with emotion, indicates his thanks to Mr. Seidl, the orchestra, and the audience, whereupon he disappears into the background while the symphony continues. After the conclusion of the work he is called for with stormy insistence. He bows again and again and ever new storms of applause break out. And even when he has left his box and entered the foyer, the clapping continues. At last he returns to the gallery. With what enthusiasm he is greeted! The whole orchestra and Mr. Seidl are clapping too...

From a notice in the New York Herald (17. XII. 1893), a paper which showed a special interest in Dvořák and his work.

172. DVOŘÁK DELIGHTED AT THE SYMPHONY'S SUCCESS

... The success of the symphony was tremendous; the papers write that no composer has ever had such success. I was in a box; the hall was filled with the best New York audience, the people clapped so much that I had to thank them from the box like a king!? alla *Mascagni* in Vienna (don't laugh!). You know how glad I am if I can avoid such ovations, but there was no getting out of it, and I had to show myself willy-nilly. Seidl said he would wire you about the success. I shall have two more performances—on the 23rd and on the 31st December. *Paur* of Leipzig is conducting... I am happy and congratulate you and myself that the work is being published by your firm. The Quartet and Quintet will be given next week...

Dvořák to Simrock in Berlin, 20. XII. 1893.—The Italian composer, *Pietro Mascagni*, had earned great success in Vienna with his opera, "Cavaliera Rusticana" shortly before Dvořák's departure for America.—*Emil Pauer*, successor to Arthur Nikisch in the direction of the Boston Symphony Orchestra.—Dvořák's String Quartet in F major, op. 96, was first performed by the Kneisel Quartet (see 161) in Boston on New Year's Day 1894 and again, along with the String Quintet in E flat major, op. 97, and the Sextet, op. 48, on the 12th January of the same year, in the Carnegie Hall in New York (see also 174).

173. DVOŘÁK HOMESICK FOR BOHEMIA

... At the urgent request of brother-in-law Dvořák, I take the liberty of troubling you after some time with a few lines. He begs his dear friend to write to him at least once and is longing for a letter from you; you know very well, he says, that of all his friends you are the dearest and just for that reason he longs to get some little note which would give him such pleasure. Please be so good as to fulfil his ardent wish. In spite of his splendid position and material prosperity he is terribly homesick for his country. Dvořák and Otla miss home most of all.

On my departure from New York, when they all accompanied me on board, Dvořák broke into tears and said: "If I could, I should go with you and were it only between-decks."

*From a letter from Dvořák's sister-in-law, Mrs. Koutecká (*see 161*), to Alois Göbl at Sychrov (*see 33*). New York 25. II. 1894.*

174. CONCERTS AND NEW WORKS

Dear Friend,   New York, 18 27/2 94.

Three cheers for you!

At last after 1 1/2 years your long and longingly awaited letter arrived. And how excited I was! And not only I—all of us—Otilka and Mother came running downstairs, I sat down in the sitting-room and played—"What is it?" and "Where is it from?" What a calling out there was—and I—from Sychrov! With what impatience and happy anticipation I opened your letter. You have given me great pleasure, more than you know and I thank you from my heart for this, I might almost say—surprise. From your letter I see that you know about us, what and how we are doing here.

Thanks be to God we are well and we do not worry about anything else, though I often have troubles enough, but one must overcome them. As you see, in spite of my work at school, I have been fairly diligent. I have written a symphony which has created quite a furore in America, but besides that I have written a Quartet for strings and a Quintet with two violas. The Quartet is in F major and the Quintet in E flat. In January there was a "Dvořák Evening" given by an excellent quartet from Boston (the Kneisel Quartet). In addition they also played the sextet—the audience was again as enthusiastic as at the Symphony. I sat with my wife among the audience and during the evening I had to rise from my seat several times and thank the audience for giving my new works such a splendid reception. I can, without hesitation, count these three works as my best and most original. All the critics are of the same opinion and one paper, the New York Daily Herald, wrote in so many words: "Why did not Dvořák come to us earlier if he can write such music here in America?"

Besides a Sonatina for violin, I am just finishing a new work —"Suite" for piano. Perhaps you do not know that I am on good terms again with Simrock. He has bought *everything I had* and *wants all* my new things.

All three Overtures are out as I learn from the newspapers here. The "Dumky" too,—and the Rondo for 'cello—*Brahms himself* was kind enough to correct the proofs and I must thank him for doing so. He wrote to Simrock that he sends me his greetings and has heart-felt pleasure in my "fröhliches Schaffen" —as he writes in his letter to Simrock. The Symphony, Quartet and Quintet have also been bought by Simrock—but these will probably not come out till summer. I shall see to it that you get all these compositions—perhaps I may even hand them to you personally in summer, for I intend to make the trip to Bohemia this year, but of that I shall tell you more later.—We should leave (all of us) about the 15th and could be in Prague by the 26th May...

With a warm embrace and greetings,
Your devoted
Antonín Dvořák.

Will you be writting soon? I shall—

Dvořák to A. Göbl at Sychrov.—For the concert given by the Kneisel Quartet see 172.—Other new compositions written in New York: *Sonatina in G major for Violin and Piano,* composed between October 19th and December 3rd 1893. Dvořák dedicated it, as the jubilee opus 100, to his children Otilie and Antonín.—The piano *Suite in A major,* published as op. 98, was composed in February 1894.

19. S. S. Saale on which Dvořák sailed to America and returned again to Europe three years later.

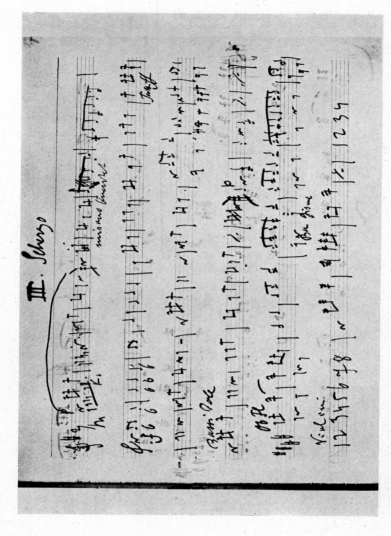

20. Facsimile of a page from the sketch for the Symphony "From the New World".

126–128 East 17th Street,
New York, 18 2/4 94.

Dear Dr. Tragy,

I know that I am probably in your bad books for being so
long in replying as there was nothing I could tell you for certain. Only now can I say that (God willing) we shall soon see
each other in Prague. We have berths reserved on the boat
which sails from New York on the 19th May and so we hope
to be in Prague at the end of May. Then I shall have so much
to tell you that I shall be dinging your ears with my talk.
Some newspapers announced that I had signed a contract
for two years—but it is not true. Whether I shall remain or
not I do not know yet—but we shall talk of that when I get
to Prague.

You are sure to have read about my Symphony in the
papers. It was a great triumph and it is now in the press (Simrock has bought all my compositions and again wants new ones).
You were right that he would come and not I.—I have also
written a new Quartet in F major and a Quintet in E flat for
strings (also in the press) then I have written a Sonatina (for my
children) for violin and piano, then a Suite for piano and 10
Songs from the Holy Bible, "David's Psalms".

So you see I have been busy enough and am, God be thanked,
well and in good spirits. Recently Simrock wrote me that Brahms
had mentioned me in one of his letters and said:

*Sagen Sie dem Dvořák, daß ich ihn herzlich grüße und daß ich
mich über sein fröhliches Schaffen sehr freue.*

He was so kind, you must know, as to correct all my
compositions such as the Overtures and the "Dumky"—that is
he went through all the proofs from Leipzig and corrected the
misprints, which is the most tedious work a composer knows—
but to my great surprise Brahms, with remarkable unselfishness,

took over this task. That is about all I have to tell you today—
the rest in Prague. God bless you and

> au revoir, Your deeply obliged and devoted

Antonín Dvořák.

It is already half past eight and the packet-ship *Havel* sails at seven in the morning for Europe, so I must hurry and post the letter.

> *Dvořák to Dr. Tragy* (see 133) *in Prague.*—Dvořák kept to the date of departure here indicated and arrived with his whole family in Prague on the 30th May 1894. After a short stay he left for his favourite summer residence of Vysoká.—10 Songs from the Holy Bible, "David's Psalms": *Biblical Songs* with piano accompaniment, op. 99 written in March 1894.

176. ON THE EVE OF DEPARTURE

New York, 18 20/4 94.

Dear Friend Simrock,

I expect you know what happened to the s. s. *Ems* on the crossing. Having sailed from Bremen on March 17th, she was damaged on the 23rd at sea, but was fortunately sighted by a small ship and brought to the Azores 1000 miles off her course, and so your letter and the music arrived only today, Friday, April 20th (i. e. about 5 weeks late). Many thanks for same. I am very pleased to give you more details about my new small compositions which I have just finished.

I have a Sonatina for violin and piano (easy), then a Suite for pianoforte (of medium difficulty), then 10 new Songs (2 vols.) taken from the Bible, and I think that the Suite for piano and the Songs are the best things I have done in this field. Besides these, I have a choral work (duration 20 mins.) – perhaps you could take everything. The things are sure to go very well and the cost of printing will not be so great this time. I am not sending you the things yet, but write by return so that the letter reaches me before I leave for Europe–I am sailing on the

19th May by the *"Aller"* via Bremen to Europe, and hope to be in Prague by the 28th May.

How I am looking forward to seeing my native land again! Unfortunately I shall go there with a sad heart for I shall not see my aged Father again. He died just four weeks ago!

Greetings from

Antonín Dvořák.

For the Sonatina and Suite see 174 for the Biblical Songs see 175. The choral work referred to here is the Te Deum.—Dvořák's father, František, died in Bohemia on March 28th 1894, only some days before the completion of the Biblical Songs.

177. A GIFT OF THANKSGIVING

The celebrated master of music, Dr. Antonín Dvořák, donated to the Church here a new organ which was consecrated on September 8th and dedicated to its purpose.

And I played on the organ!

Antonín Dvořák.

Entry for 8. IX. 1894 in the School Chronicle of Třebsko near Vysoká where Dvořák was fond of playing the organ at mass (see 75 and 187). The new organ for the choir of the church there was Dvořák's gift of thanksgiving for the safe return of himself and his family to Bohemia.

178. DVOŘÁK TO HIS CHILDREN

Otilka, you are the oldest and most sensible and I depend on you and also on Anička. Be good then and, Anynka, take good care of yourself so that you don't fall ill.

Go—and remember what I say—often to church, you know, Otilka, what I told you—especially on Sundays see that you go to church. Pray fervently, it is the one thing that can comfort you and us. Look to it that the others, too, Mařka and Toník, say their prayers—I am not worrying about Zičinka, she will do it

all right, the good little soul. More next time. I thank you, Grandma, for everything, and commend you to God's keeping.
Your Loving Father and Mother,

Antonín Dvořák.

From a letter written to the children in Prague on his second journey to America in October 1894.—After the summer holidays spent peacefully in the summer retreat at Vysoká, Dvořák with his wife and younger son, Otakar, left on October 16th once more for New York, which they reached on October 25th. The other five children Otilie, Anna (Anička, Anynka), Magda (Mařka), Aloisie (Zičinka) and Antonín remained in Prague.

179. SAFE ARRIVAL

New York,
Monday 29th Oct. 1894.

Dear Friend,

I know that you have always been a dear and rare friend and so I wish to write to you knowing that it will give you a little pleasure.

Now I shall tell you first of all that we got safely to this country of America and that our journey was quite agreeable except for about two days—when it was so stormy that only very few were not affected by seasickness—and I was among the lucky few, so that we may thank God that it fell out so fortunately.

We travelled on the *Bismarck* from Hamburg. She is a fine ship and crossed the immense ocean, 3100 miles (not including the 450 miles from Hamburg to Southampton), in 6 days, 10 hours and some minutes, so that we anchored before New York on Thursday, the 25th October at 8 o'clock in the evening.

We have been here only 3 days and so I have not really any news for you—I shall leave it for next time. In the meanwhile accept my kind regards to yourself and your wife,

Yours affectionately,

Antonín Dvořák.

Dvořák to Adolf Heyduk (1835-1923), a distinguished Czech poet, to whose verses Dvořák composed the "Gipsy Melodies", op. 55 (see 44). The letter was addressed to Písek in Bohemia where Heyduk was a professor at the Realgymnasium.

180. AT WORK AGAIN IN NEW YORK

By the s. s. *Teutonie* via England.

New York, 18 18/12 94.

Dear Friend,

It is quite a long time since I wrote to you—and as I have not had any word from you, I think you must not have got my first letter from New York.

We are well, God be praised, but this time we do not feel so at ease as last year. We were used to the children and now we haven't them and are sad at having to be without them. Otherwise everything would be all right.

And how about you?—everything all right? I am thinking chiefly about whether you are in good health. You often used to be all together on Sundays and then I always remember you and think how happy I should be to be with you and among you!

The children write to us twice a week and we always await the ships coming from Europe expectantly in the hope that they have brought us something. And when a letter does come from the children, you can imagine with what impatience we seize it and read it.

They write that they are well and getting on nicely—only Otla always writes how glad she would be to see us again in Prague. I believe her—and we the same.

In the musical world there is plenty going on here. The New York Philharmonic presented me with an honorary diploma as an honorary member and played my new Symphony not long ago. In January again they will play all three Overtures. The Symphony has been given in Chicago and many other towns and everywhere it was a success.

The "Lužany Mass", which I composed at the request of Mr. Hlávka—in the year 1887 (if I am not mistaken)—this mass will be given at Christmas here in New York at the Catholic Church of St. Stephen, and then in other towns such as Saint Paul, where we were last year, in Minneapolis, in New Orleans etc. And now I have still to tell you that I am working at a concerto for violoncello. But I must not forget the chief thing: A New Year is coming round again and greetings. I wish you from my heart every good thing and especially health and contentment and God grant that we shall see each other in the coming year and that we shall be as good friends as we have always been, which is the heartfelt wish of

Your devoted friend,

Antonín Dvořák.

Dvořák to Ant. Rus (see 81) in Písek.—"The Lužany Mass": the Mass in D major, op. 86 (see 112).—Dvořák composed the famous *Concerto for Violoncello and Orchestra in B minor,* op. 104, between the 8th November 1894 and the 9th February 1895 in New York. It was the only work to be composed in this season and was the composer's song of immeasurable longing and yearning for his native country.

181. MUSICAL EVENTS IN NEW YORK

... Now I am finishing the Finale of the Violoncello Concerto.

If I could work as free from cares as at Vysoká, it would have been finished long ago. But here it is not possible—on Monday I have work at school—on Tuesday I am free—the other days are more of less taken up—in short I cannot give so much time to my work, and when I could, again I am not always in the mood etc.

In short, the best thing is to sit at Vysoká—there I have the best recreation, the best refreshment—and am happy. Oh if only I were there again!

I think that "In Nature's Realm" will not find favour in Vienna—but what can you do? Everything is not for everybody and everybody is not for everything...

The Boston Kneisel Quartet has already given its 50th performance of the F major Quartet. Not bad, is it?

Only last week it was given here, and again it was a great

success—for the overtures, on the other hand, they have not as yet the same understanding.

All three were played here by the Philharmonic. Seidl conducted extremely well—and the critics say they do not understand them—the programme namely, what I thought and meant by them! But almost nothing about the music! Only always about the programme etc. Seidl and the orchestra like them very well and that is enough in the meanwhile.

If you can, write again soon—

With kindest regards, Your

Antonín Dvořák.

Dvořák in New York to Josef Boleška, composer, in Prague, 15. I. 1895.—For the Kneisel Quartet see 161.—The three Overtures: see 157.

182. HOME FOR GOOD

Dear Friend,
Vysoká, 30/7 95.

I should like to go to Lužany again in the first days of September. I cannot stay longer than the 14th—I must be at home.

So arrange it as it suits you best.

Ferdinand Hellmesberger wrote me that the Vienna Philharmonic wishes to play the Concerto and that he would be the soloist. I am just writing to him. I do not know anything for certain yet, whether it will be possible, as Simrock has not written me. So I cannot tell you anything definite either.

We shall leave the other news for Lužany. Since I have come back from America I have not put pen to paper, and so the new quartet begun in New York is still not finished.

The first movement unfinished and of the others not even the beginnings!—Here at Vysoká I grudge the time and prefer to enjoy the beauties of the countryside.

Give my kind regards to Mr. Hoffman and Mr. Nedbal and to Mr. Suk—

Au revoir in Lužany— Yours,

Antonín Dvořák.

Do you not know where Ondříček is?
and when he is going to America?
or if he is going at all?

Dvořák at Vysoká to the violoncellist, Hanuš Wihan (see 157).—Lužany see 112.— Ferdinand Hellmesberger, violoncellist, son of Josef H. (see 36).—The new quartet: *String Quartet in A flat major, op. 105,* of which Dvořák wrote part of the first movement in New York (March 1895), but the rest in Prague in December of the same year. — The well-known violinist, František Ondříček (see 62), went in 1895 on a six-months concert tour of America.

183. DVOŘÁK ADAMANT ON THE CELLO CONCERTO

Prague, 3. 10. 95.

Dear Mr. Simrock,

The copyist is not finished yet, but next week everything will be ready. I have had some differences of opinion with Friend Wihan on account of a number of places. I do not like some of the passages—and I must insist on my work being printed as I have written it. The passages in question can be printed in two versions, an *easier* and a *more difficult* version. I shall only then give you the work if you promise not to allow *anybody* to make changes—Friend Wihan not excepted—without my *knowledge* and *consent*—and also not the Cadenza which Wihan has added to the last movement. There is no Cadenza in the last movement either in the score or in the piano arrangement. I told Wihan straight away when he showed it me that it was impossible to stick such a bit on. The finale closes gradually diminuendo—like a sigh—with reminiscences of the I. and II. movements—the solo dies down to pp (—then swells again—)

and the last bars are taken up by the orchestra and the whole concludes in stormy mood. — That was my idea and I cannot depart from it. If then you agree to these conditions, including the printing of the titles also in Czech, I am willing to give you the Concerto and the Te Deum together for 6000M (six thousand marks).

With kind regards,

Ant. Dvořák.

Dvořák to Simrock, 3. X. 1895. — Prof. Hanuš Wihan (see 157).

184. THE BOHEMIAN QUARTET AND DVOŘÁK

With Antonín Dvořák is closely bound up my own artistic life and that of the Bohemian Quartet, for it is filled with the artistic treasures of our teacher and master on which was built up the existence of our Quartet. With them the Bohemian Quartet harvested its greatest successes both at home and abroad—successes which, for us, are linked up with the subjective experiences and impressions derived from the Master's compositions and from the reception which was given them everywhere we appeared. And today, when we still return to Dvořák, again and again, we are filled with the proud and happy consciousness that it was we who, during our studies at the Conservatoire, gazed with respect and bated breath into his face, that we were near him, that we were allowed to sink our attention in the magic circle of his deep and fiery eyes and that to us it was vouchsafed to observe and to admire from close at hand and in all its aspects his simple but great and noble spirit. We could scarcely have foreseen that we should soon have the good fortune to stand in a still closer relationship to our Master.

Dvořák it was, and again Dvořák, who became, with the great number of his chamber works, the principal source of our

185

programmes, so that we still play Dvořák, today; nor has his work lost for us any of its freshness, we play it with the same emotion and love as we did for the first time, and we feel that our relation to him has finally matured to one of lasting admiration and gratitude. And we feel the same attitude to him among the audiences of all nations; everywhere the same enthusiasm and still unabated interest when his free movements sing forth the divine spirit of great genius, everywhere the same delight in movement and rhythm, everywhere the same admiration and respect for his amazing craftsmanship and invention. In his works, the originality of his Slav soul exults, in other places, weeps, everywhere exacting from the audience its tribute os unfeigned admiration. And so with Dvořák we achieve succesy after success, and in growing measure, and are consummatelf happy in the conviction that though the present time is seeking a new music and new trends for its expression, Antonín Dvořák remains for us and for the world one of the Immortals.

From *"Dvořák in the Recollections of the Bohemian Quartet"* by the leader of the Quartet, *Karel Hoffman* (1872-1936).

185. DVOŘÁK ON THE CREATIVE PROCESS

... How do you work out your ideas, Master?—

"Gluck is said to have affirmed that he has his opera complete in his head before he writes it. I do not know if that is right, but to a certain extent I find it is true of myself. I always make sketches which contain the substance of the motifs for my work, the basic material for the intended musical expression. After a period of intense thought, of conscious concentration of my artistic 'I', the work proceeds smoothly and quickly. My imagination requires to be stimulated but then it carries me

186

along with it... I work relatively little, only in the forenoons.
I do not work long, for when I do work, I do it at a stretch.
It does not tire me."

From an interview "*Bei Meister Dvořák*", published in the German daily, "Politik" (26. XI. 1899), by *Egon Šamberk*.

186. DVOŘÁK'S METHODS OF WORK

... The Master, who was a tireless worker, at once fell into a
bad mood if he was without employment. He was more or less
irritable, bad-tempered, distraught, there was, so to speak, no
making anything of him, sometimes the most trifling question
put him in a fury, sometimes he answered but more often he did
not answer at all; and so it was, always, when his mind was taken
up and his thoughts concentrated on a new work.

No sooner, however, was the future work decided upon,
his thoughts collected and work started than the Master was
quite a different creature; absorbed in his work, he took no heed
whether the earth turned from east to west or the other way
about, worked calmly and contentedly, was glad when his work
went forward satisfactorily, and if, as he was in the habit of
saying, "he brought something off", then he was in a particularly
good mood; a truly delightful person, always smiling and
joking; and if it happened that anybody came to the Master at
such a time with some request, no matter what,—none went away
unheard and if it was a matter of financial support–the Master
emptied his pocket to the last heller–a proceeding to which
I was often a witness.

From the Memoirs of Josef J. Kovařík (see 158).

187. LIFE AT VYSOKÁ

During his summer stay at Vysoká, Dvořák used to go for a walk in the park and woods early every morning and often he would wake us up at 5 o'clock and be surprised that we could sleep when the thrushes were holding their morning concert above our heads. Often he went to the Kounices and then came to me at the gamekeeper's lodge, and besides he was fond of walking in the fields, being often accompanied on his rambles by one of the local teachers, Dražan, of whom he was very fond.

In the evening he used to go to the inn which was frequented by miners and here he would tell them about his sojourn in America which greatly interested them. He was also fond of going to the neighbouring village of Střebsko, to the parish church, where he liked to play the organ he had gifted to the church in thanksgiving for his safe return and that of his family from America.

In the winter all was quiet at Vysoká and work went on in the woods, but when spring passed into summer, when Mr. and Mrs. Kounic arrived and the Dvořák family, things became lively at Vysoká. In a little villa at the edge the wood, the poet Sládek, for many years spent the summer with his wife and daughter, Helenka. Nearly every day they all met at our place, at the Dvořáks' or in front of the Kounic's villa. The Dvořáks were always having visitors, Suk, Nedbal, the young Czecho-American, Kovařík, the American, Hopkins, and many, many others, so that it was very gay and noisy, and then Dvořák usually disappeared into the woods for peace and quiet.

He liked, too, to sit in the courtyard where he would watch for hours a flock of lovely pigeons — his pride and delight.

Many of his works he would bring, maybe in the morning, to play over to us, and we keep the piano on which he used to play as a cherished souvenir.

From a letter by Jan Hertan (1860-1943), head gamekeeper at Vysoká, whose wife was Mrs. Dvořák's youngest sister. — *Hopkins,* an American who studied under Dvořák in Prague.

188. DVOŘÁK – PIGEON-FANCIER

Vysoká by Příbram

Dear Sir,

Please forgive me for being so long in writing to thank you for the lovely gift with which you have given me such very great pleasure. My reason for not writing was that I wanted to know whether these beautiful pigeons would settle. I waited long till at last my efforts were rewarded. The French ones took their time about it—they showed no inclination to go into the dovecote with the other pigeons and only yesterday we put the "black tiger" with the black pigeon, so that I think everything is all right and there will be no more trouble.

It was really comical, I can tell you. The whole day I was running from one cottage to another in the village for fear the "Frenchies" might fly away. Everybody who passes by stops to look at the lovely creatures. All the pigeon-fanciers here are talking about them. Accept then my warmest thanks for this delightful gift.

I remain, Your obliged and devoted

Antonín Dvořák.

Dvořák to Jindřich Strniště, director of the choir and choirmaster in Třebíč in Moravia, who was also a great lover of pigeons and had given Dvořák a gift of some rare birds.

189. DVOŘÁK'S LOVE OF THE COMMON PEOPLE

... With his fine but unassuming nature, he inclined mainly to the common people from whom he had sprung. I often used to see him in the country inn at Vysoká playing "darda" with the neighbours or talking with them about pigeons and farming in general. Of these neighbours he was fondest of the farmer and mayor, Mr. Fencl. A curious thing was that though he scarcely ever talked about music and then only with reluctance, he talked music very often with this neighbour and, as I learned later, invited him to Prague at his own expense, took him to the National Theatre to see one of his own operas, and having shown him all proper hospitality, graciously sent him home again.

Once on the Master's name-day, the village musicians from Třebsko, Vysoká and Bohutín came to play a "Standerl" in his honour, having previously diligently practised some "opera" pieces in order to please the Master. The Master thanked them and invited them into the inn where he treated them and then got them to play him some village music, whereupon he said to the musicians: "Look, play me these things, that's what I like, and these opera pieces—leave them to others!"

From Reminiscences by Bohumil Fidler (see 75).

190. DVOŘÁK'S OTHER PASTIMES

Something that is perhaps quite unknown to the general public is that Father was very keen on gymnastics which at first consisted in taking a chair and doing arm exercises with it. Later he got himself dumb bells and exercised with them early in the morning. He was also something of a sportsman. His sport was skittles at Vysoká. Almost every Sunday forenoon, and usually Thursday afternoon as well, was devoted to a game of skittles, in an alley situated at the foot of the garden. The set of skittles is still kept at Vysoká as a much-prized souvenir.

From Reminiscences by Dvořák's younger son, Otakar.

191. VISITS TO BRAHMS AND RICHTER IN VIENNA

Dearest Friend,

We are all, thanks be to God, well and rejoice to be able, after three years, to spend a happy and joyous Christmas in Bohemia! How different it was for us last year in America, when we were far away in foreign parts and separated from all our children and friends! But God has been pleased to grant us this happy moment and so we all feel inexpressibly glad!

I am now working very hard. I work so easily and everything goes ahead so well that I could not wish it better. I have just finished a new G major quartet and now again am finishing a second in A flat major. Two movements are quite complete and I am just writing the Andante, and expect to be finished with after the holidays.

I must also tell you that I was in Vienna with my wife a week ago. Brahms was tremendously pleased. We were together nearly all the time. I went to see Richter and played over the E minor Symphony to him. He will give it at the 6th concert (about the end of February) and I must go there for it.

You say you are coming to Prague? Cannot you come to the Philharmonic Concert on the 4th January? It would be so nice. I shall be conducting the A flat Rhapsody, Othello, then the Symphony and the Biblical Songs with a small orchestra. Arrange it so that you can come.

Greetings from us all,

Your affectionate friend,

A. Dvořák.

Dvořák to A. Göbl (see 34) *at Sychrov.—String Quartet in G major,* op. 106, was composed between the beginning and the 28th of November 1895, earlier than the *A flat major Quartet* begun in New York (see 182) and finished on the 30th December of the same year. Both works were the expression of the joy felt by Dvořák at his return for good to his beloved homeland.—The Symphony referred to is the "From the New World", which was performed by Richter with the Vienna Philharmonic on the 16th February 1896.—At the concert of the Czech Philharmonic held in Prague on January 4th 1896, Dvořák conducted the III. Slavonic Rhapsody, the Biblical Songs with orchestra, the "Othello" Overture and the "From the New World" Symphony.

192. VIENNA AND THE "NEW WORLD SYMPHONY"

... I was in Vienna on the 16th February 1896. Richter sent me a telegram. It was a great success and the audience gave me a grand reception. I sat with Brahms in the Director's box.— The applause was so great that I had to bow from the box three times after the Largo and again three times after the Scherzo, and after the Finale I had to go down into the hall, and show myself to the appreciative audience from the platform. I have never known such a success in Vienna. I thank God for it!

Your

Ant. Dvořák.

Dvořák to Simrock in Berlin, 19. II. 1896.—See 191.

193. DVOŘÁK - BRAHMS - BRUCKNER

... Dvořák was seized with a sudden longing to see Brahms and went with us once to Vienna. It happened that on that occasion we played, on one evening, three masterpieces of new chamber music: the B flat major Sextet by Brahms, the A major Sextet by Dvořák and a Quintet by Bruckner. I went with Dvořák and his wife to visit Brahms and it is a visit I shall never forget. Brahms tried to persuade Dvořák to move to Vienna and because he knew that he had a big family, he said: "Look here, Dvořák, you have a lot of children and I haven't almost anybody. If you need anything, my fortune is at your disposal." The tears came into Mrs. Dvořák's eyes and Dvořák, deeply touched, seized the Master's hand. Then the conversation turned to faith and religion. Dvořák, as is well known, was possessed of a sincere and almost child-like faith, whereas Brahms's views were quite the opposite. "I have read a lot of Schopenhauer and look on things differently," he remarked... On the way back to the hotel, Dvo-

21. School and church in Spillville, America.

22. The Kneisel Quartet in Boston.

řák was more than usually silent. At last after some considerable time he exclaimed: "Such a man, such a soul—and he doesn't believe in anything, he doesn't believe in anything!" A few days later, Dvořák received from Brahms Sabatier's book "St. Francis" in which he then read diligently.

On the evening on which the Bruckner Quintet was to be performed, we went before the concert to visit Bruckner and invite him to the performance of his work. At that time Bruckner occupied the well-known vaulted room in the Belvedere. We found him with his coat off at his writing desk and we had the impression that this was the home of a man who lives altogether in the world of the spirit and for his work. He looked at us without a sign of recognition, with a far-away look in his eyes and did not at once grasp what we were wanting. Only after a while did he comprehend: "You want me to come to the concert. I can't do that. I am so often ailing and I have too much work. You see I am busy working at the Adagio of the 9th and so I must stay at home today." When we took leave of him he was suddenly very touched. Tears stood in those remarkable eyes of his. He saw us out in his quilted vest and blew us kisses as long as our carriage remained in sight.

Josef Suk (see 1): "*Aus meiner Jugend*", Wiener Brahms-Erinnerungen. (Published in the Viennese musical magazine "Der Merker" II.).—The visit to Brahms and to Bruckner took place on the 27th March, 1896, the day of the concert in Vienna by the Bohemian Quartet. It is not known whether Dvořák also went to see Bruckner.—Bruckner died on the 11th October 1896.

194. A TRAVEL REMINISCENCE

. . . In the meantime we, along with Dvořák, had reached the "Pálavské hory". "What is that?—I never noticed it before. What a curious thing!" I told him all I knew about the hills, about where you go to climb them, I mentioned the legend—but the Master no longer seemed to be listening. Knowing his way,

I was sure that he was turning something over in his mind and that in a little while he would come out with something original—the result of his cogitations. I was just beginning to think I had been mistaken, but in a little the Master began: "I always envied Wagner that he could write. Where would I be today if I could write! And I can't speak either.—But listen," and he raised his voice under the stress of some strong emotion, "if I could speak I should call our nation here and I should climb up that hill and from there I should tell them something, and tell it them straight, but I can't speak". And then he relapsed once more into silence and for long gazed out from the carriage at the "Pálavské hory".

From "Reminiscences of Master Dvořák" by Karel Sázavský (1858-1930), Czech musical critic and secretary to the Philharmonic Society "Beseda Brněnská".—Sázavský accompanied Dvořák on the return journey from Vienna via Brno to Prague from the visit described above.—"Pálavské hory", now called "Vrchy Pavlovské" in the south of Moravia.

195. DVOŘÁK'S SILENCE

Once on a Sunday forenoon we met at Velebin Urbánek's shop. Dvořák invited me to go to a wine-shop. I was not accustomed at that time to drink anything in the forenoon and was not very willing to comply. But Dvořák insisted: "Please do me the favour, I should not go alone." So I said I would and we sat down in Masaryk's little Moravian wine-shop. I began a conversation several times but Dvořák did not reply. I recalled his recent visit to Písek. And still Dvořák remained silent. So I fell silent, too, and we sat opposite each other without a word. When Dvořák had finished his glass, we paid and went out. In the street he shook me warmly by the hand and said: "You don't know how grateful I am that you went with me; you have done me a great service," and we parted...

From "Musical Memoirs" by Ladislav Dolanský (see 73).—Velebín Urbánek see 50.

196. DVOŘÁK'S CREATIVE CREDO

... "That would be lovely," exclaimed one of the pupils enthusiastically. "Of course it would be lovely," rejoined the Master sharply, "but the thing is *to do it*". The last words were pronounced with such emphasis that it was almost a shout. He immediately, however, moderated his tone and continued calmly:

"To have a lovely thought is nothing so remarkable. A thought comes of itself and if it is fine and great it is not our merit. *But to carry out a thought well and make something great of it, that is the most difficult thing, that is, in fact*–art! How often a thought seems simple at first sight but in carrying it out such difficulties arise–I call them 'knots'–that you can't untie them, not if you were to do I don't know what. I, for instance, would like to compose the 'Nazareth' and 'Golgotha' and, with God's help, maybe I should manage to do it so that I should be pleased with it and others, too. But who would write the text for me? We have, it is true, some excellent poets but I know that not one of them would write it *as I should wish to have it and as I should need it*. I once said to Vrchlický that I should like to have long words of one syllable at the end of the lines and he told me that he did not know where to get them from. I have often thought about it and *I am sorry that I am not a poet myself. If I could write poetry, I should write the text myself and, in between writing the verses, I should know how it would look in the score!*..."

From "My First Lesson With Dvořák" by Josef Michl (see 4).

197. FIRST PERFORMANCE OF THE VIOLONCELLO CONCERTO

My dear, good Friend,   Prague, 18 10/4 96.

... Seeing you have read in the newspaper about my Vienna concert, there is no need to write anything further about it. It turned out wonderfully, and that's that. That it came off well in London, too, goes without saying. The 'Cello Concerto was a great success and Mr. Stern, who is performing the Concerto tomorrow here in Prague, played my composition to my complete satisfaction, though here and there I should have liked it a little different—but one must not be so finical and must be glad to find somebody to play the Concerto at all. If I were to tell you the whole story connected with Mr. Stern it would cover I don't know how many sheets of paper. Before I left for London, on March 14th, Mr. Stern came from Leipzig to Prague—he was here over a fortnight and lived at considerable expense at a hotel —I worried at him more than enough—I couldn't help it—he did everything very willingly and worked with enthusiasm. We studied and practised every day—and still it wasn't what I wanted—he was quite in despair and I always insisting that it was good but that it must be still better and then it really was. When I saw that it was going all right at last, I said: "We'll away to London and you shall play!" He was overjoyed and we went. That it turned out a success you will probably have read in the newspapers. The German "Politika" carried a number of notices and now, since Mr. Stern has returned to Prague, I have a whole heap that he brought me. I shall tell you about everything when we see each other. You probably know about the two String Quartets I have written and now I am finishing the Symphonic Poem (The Golden Spinning-Wheel). "The Water-Goblin" and "The Noonday Witch" are already in Benewitz's hands and they will perform all three compositions at the private musical evening which is to be held. I hope that you, too, will be there to hear the new things I have written.

Till then au revoir from a full heart!

Greetings from all, Your affectionate

Antonín Dvořák.

Dvořák to A. Göbl at Sychrov.—For the Vienna concert see 192.—*The Concerto for Violoncello in B minor* was first performed at a concert of Dvořák's works by the Philharmonic Society in London on March 19th 1896, on this, his ninth and last visit to England, at which the composer conducted also the G major Symphony and the Biblical

Songs. The solo part of the Concerto was played by the English violoncellist, *Leo Stern*, a native of Brighton (1862-1904) who again played the Concerto at the concert of the Czech Philharmonic in Prague on April 11th 1896, which Dvořák also conducted. *The Symphonic Poems* based on the Ballads by Karel Jaromír Erben (see 84) were: "*The Water-Goblin*", op. 107, composed between January 6th and February 11th, 1896; "*The Noonday Witch*", op. 108, composed in February and "*The Golden Spinning-Wheel*", composed between March 4th and April 25th of the same year. All three works were performed for the first time by the orchestra of the Prague Conservatoire in Prague, on June 3rd 1896, under the baton of Director *Antonín Bennewitz* (1833-1926).

198. INTEREST IN THE SYMPHONIC POEMS

Vysoká, 18 18/8 96.

Dear Mr. Simrock,

Suk is with me and is just wanting to go Příbram to catch the Prague train and had a letter for you with him which, however, I am holding back as, at this very moment, a messenger has just arrived from Příbram with your letter.

First of all kindly tell me when the Symphonic Poems are likely to be out. Hans Richter writes me from Bayreuth asking when the parts will be ready. I promised him in Vienna that he would be among the first to present these things to the musical world. You know what this man means for me and it would be in my interest and in yours if you could manage to get the things out as soon as possible. He asks me if he is to include them in his programme for London (November) and Vienna and he is going to Paris, too. He wants to conduct my works. So tell me, please, immediately so that I can write to him.

Our Bendl is seriously ill. I was wired for by Wihan to come to his bedside and returned from Prague yesterday. He is one of my oldest friends, in my young days he was of great help to me and made me familiar with Beethoven's symphonies, and for that I must be grateful to him—God grant he may recover!

With kind regards,

Ant. Dvořák.

Dvořák to Simrock in Berlin.—The printing of the first three Symphonic Poems was delayed till the end of 1896.—The composer, *Karel Bendl* (see 16).

199. DVOŘÁK'S REPLY

Vysoká by Příbram, 20. 8. 1896.

My esteemed Friend,

Your letter directed to me in Prague reached me with some delay so I hasten to reply to your requests straight away. My three Symphonic Poems are being printed by Mr. Simrock. As he writes to me, today, he cannot fix an exact date but assures me that they will be ready by November, and that he, himself, will inform you.

As soon as I get the proofs, I shall tell you how the matter stands.

I laid special stress in my letter to Mr. Simrock on how important I consider it that you should perform these works and as soon as possible. I remember very well (and I must say at once with gratitude) how, after the first performance of my Rhapsody in A flat major in the year 1879, under your direction, that composition went the round of the musical world.

And this time, too, I have the highest hopes. These three compositions are from our folk-lore. They are entitled: 1. "The Water-Goblin", 2. "The Noonday Witch" and 3. "The Golden Spinning-Wheel".

I am looking forward like a child to hearing these compositions conducted by you.

You write to me something about Paris. In this connection, I should beg you to choose my E minor Symphony "From the New World". It would be a good choice I think for Paris, but I do not wish in any way to dictate. Only, should you wish to play any of my symphonies, then this is the one I should prefer.

One more thing—Could you let me know when you have your concerts in London? I must write to Simrock about it.

With warmest greetings,

Your devoted and ever grateful

Antonín Dvořák.

Dvořák to Hans Richter in Bayreuth.—For the performance of the III. Slavonic Rhapsody in A flat major under Richter's baton see 37.—At his concert with the Colonne Orchestra in Paris, Richter gave only the "Carnival" Overture and not till the 3rd April 1898. He conducted the "From the New World" Symphony, however, at the Philharmonic Concert in Budapest on the 9th February 1896, and again, in London, on the 4th June of the same year.

200. RICHTER PRESSES FOR DISPATCH OF SYMPHONIC POEMS

Dear Friend,

As a postscript to my telegram I must ask you to urge Simrock very strongly to send the score and parts to London to reach me by the 16th October at the latest and to address them: N. Vert, 6, Cork Street, Burlington Gardens, London W.— I *must* have the music by the 16th for I have only two rehearsals for the London concert, the best guarantee that your work will be well studied as the rest of the programme consists of well-known works so that I shall have the whole time at my disposal for the novelty. On the 20th we are going to the Provinces, where we shall perform your work in all the big towns: Liverpool, Manchestrer, Birmingham, Leeds, Brighton, Glasgow, Edinburgh, Nottingham, Oxford and Newcastle; after the success of which I personally have no doubt, the Societies of these towns will also hasten to acquire this novelty. It is then *in Simrock's own interest* if it is ready in time. If he doesn't send me the parts in time, I shall lose six provincial towns and shall have only one rehearsal. I want, however, to gain a complete victory…So, please put pressure on Simrock.

My warm thanks for your sincere words of appreciation. Believe me, too, that I have a warm interest in your works and that I always apply myself with enthusiasm to their study and performance. It was so, is so and shall be so. At the 2. or 3. Philharmonic Concert, I shall then present the work here in Vienna. And here I must at once insist that you take up your

abode this time, along with Madam, your wife, at Hotel Richter—
and no excuses!—

When can I have the score of your work, if even only for a
week. For 1. I must study it and 2. I must write out the principal
motifs for Barry for his programme notes, and, what is important,
let me know in this connection what are your wishes and send
your own explanatory notes. Should you wish to telegraph,
then only: Hofoper, Vienna is enough.

Awaiting your favourable answer,

I am, with best regards, Your ever devoted

Hans Richter.

I shall also conduct the new work in Budapest as I am conducting the Philharmonic Concerts there. Simrock will make a
fortune out of me, i. e. out of my zeal for you, dear Friend.

The delay in printing the music (see 199) prevented Richter from carrying out
his intention to perform Dvořák's Symphonic Poems on his concert tour in England.—
Charles A. Barry, director of vocal recitals in London, editor of the "Monthly Musical
Record" and music critic of the "London News".—Richter speaks consistently of one
composition in the erroneous idea that all three Symphonic Poems form a single work.

201. THE DEVIL AND KATE

The friendly dwelling of our celebrated Master as yet
untouched by any modern refinements of comfort is, as you
may know, in Žitná ulice, in an old house to the right across the
courtyard, and two stairs up. A latticed door, which opens
easily to those familiar with it, shuts off the composer's family
sanctuary from the outside world. A longish passage leads to the
glass door of the flat itself.

I enter the well-known room, which is here the drawing-
room, the friendly room which, devoid of all superfluous luxury,
evokes a truly agreeable feeling in the visitor. At the right is an
open piano, then a laurel wreath, at the window a writing desk.

On the left is a drawing-room table and chairs. An ordinary carpet is surrounded by not very expensive mats. This is the "best room", the "Prunkstube" of the Czech Master whose fame fills the world...

"Master, when did the idea occur to you of composing "The Devil and Kate?"

—"This opera has a very interesting history. Once—it may be two years ago—I met Dr. Rieger. We stopped to chat and Dr. Rieger asked me: 'What are you working at?'—I replied: 'I am working very hard.' Dr. Rieger then looked into my face and inquired further: 'Wouldn't you like to compose an opera?' —'Certainly, dramatic music has a great attraction for me'. Dr. Rieger: 'Director Šubrt has a libretto by his nephew entitled The Devil and Kate. If you are interested, read it through.' —I went to 'Director Šubrt and, on reading it, was not a little attracted by it. Good friends such as V. J. Novotný, whom I asked for advice, had various objections and pointed out that the text had nothing lyrical in it and even Dr. Rieger, who took a lively interest in my new opera, was of the opinion that the opera in this respect was not suitable. I, however, considered it original and I liked it as being something entirely new. I saw in it a combination of characteristic folk and fairy-tale elements and was quite ready to forego the lyrical element, which, in this case, could be of only subordinate interest..."

From an interview with the journalist, Egon Šamberk.—The writer, *Adolf Wenig* (1874-1940), the author of the libretto "The Devil and Kate", was the nephew of the Director of the Prague National Theatre, Fr. Ad. Šubert (see 210).—*V. J. Novotný* see 2.

202. DVOŘÁK'S APPEARANCE AND MANNER

Engraved in my mind there remains – like an impression in bronze—the likeness of the great artist and his whole way of speaking. The short, broad skull, the low furrowed forehead, the eyes deep-set and luminous beneath thick black brows, the somewhat prominent cheek-bones, the reddish blunt-tipped nose and a lively mouth even when not speaking. The whole complexion very dark, a bristling moustache and a close-cut full beard, hair thin on the top but elsewhere a thick mane. And this is the picture I keep in my mind of this great creator in tone. And I always have it before my eyes in the bust which has captured the true spiritual expression of Dvořák's countenance—only stressing something here or there—as rendered by the gifted young sculptor, Josef Mařatka.

Notwithstanding the flashing of the eyes, which at times looked searchingly, almost mistrustingly, at times with the open gaze of a child, and notwithstanding the mobility of the lips, Dvořák's face had always a certain dreaminess and even meditativeness of expression. He looked as a rule very serious, rarely did he laugh. Nor did he often joke himself though he was amused by the jokes of others.

He used to come and see me at my office at the National Theatre either when he had finished some work—something new or the revision of an old work—or when rehearsals of his works were on. I do not remember him ever sitting down. He usually walked to and fro or stood at my desk or at the window, gazing into space, now in one direction, now in another, spoke or listened. And it would happen that in the middle of a sentence he would suddenly break off and become lost in thought. In his mind some musical idea had taken wing and was soaring and singing like a skylark and sometimes he straight away began to whistle it. Only after a while, and as if there had been no interruption, he would return to reality and to what he was saying. Or during a conversation about a certain subject, he would suddenly start speaking about something quite different, his mind fully occupied with it. And sometimes, in the middle of a conversation, he would turn on his heel with a greeting, or even without, and be gone. And he would maybe return in a few days "to finish what we were talking about".

That was all due to the music in him. He thought, for the most part, not in words but in tone. It was almost to be seen in his eyes and face, a constant boiling and gushing up of the geyser of sound in those innumerable melodic combinations which form the substance of his work.

From "Reminiscences" by František Adolf Šubert (1849-1915).—The noted Czech sculptor, *Josef Mařatka* (1874-1937), who, in his youth, lived in the same house as Dvořák, took the death-mask of the Master's head and hand and created his bust for the foyer of the National Theatre in Prague.

203. THE BIRTH OF A NEW OPERA

The libretto "The Devil and Kate" was not written "to order". It was finished and I did not know what its fate would be. My uncle, Director F. A. Šubert, knew from the critic, Emanuel Chvála, that Dvořák was looking for a libretto and it was through him that it was offered to the composer. It suited his purpose and he accepted it. From the character of the work, the deliberate arrangement and presentation of the material, I judged that it would meet the requirements of Dvořák's type of creative work very well. Indeed, were I to write a libretto especially for Dvořák I think I couldn't have found more suitable material. When the Master was engaged in composing the opera I went to see him quite frequently. He asked for several changes in the text but in general not of a substantial kind. Sometimes the text was too rapid in its movement and so unfavourable to the epic breadth of his musical expression...Dvořák liked to have every stage situation first explained before he completed the composition of the corresponding scene. On one occasion, when I arrived, he sat down at the piano, found a certain place in the text and in his music, and said: "And now tell me how do you picture the Devil carrying Kate on his back. It's easy enough for you to say 'on his back' but how is he going to sing at the same time?"—I explained that it would have to be merely indicated if Kate was heavy and the Devil not very robust. "All right," said the Master, and strode to the door: "So here is the gate to hell. You be the Devil and show me how he will do it." And we had a nice practical rehearsal of Kate being carried off to hell...

The librettist Adolf Wenig (see 201): "Reminiscences of a Librettist".—The opera, *"The Devil and Kate"* was composed as op. 112 between May 9th 1898 and January 29th 1899. The theme of the opera is a Czech folk-tale about a village scold who, with the help of a shrewd shepherd, tricks the Devil himself and made it hot for him even in his own Hell. Dvořák's musical conception is of a typically folk character and imbued with irresistable humour.

204. DVOŘÁK'S LAST VISIT TO BRAHMS

...Forgive me for being so long in answering but do not be surprised as I work till the evening and then I am tired and do not think about anything. Today, however, I must make an exception. I was in Vienna and visited Master Brahms, and saw how true, unfortunately, is all I heard from you. Nevertheless let us hope that all is not yet lost! God grant it may be so!...

A letter arrived today from Suk in London. His Quartet is a great success. The "Times" does not say much but is enthusiastic. Other papers, too, give the work high praise. Our Quartet make the trip every week from Holland to London and are having a good time...

Dvořák to Simrock in Berlin, 19. III. 1897.—Dvořák, having heard that Brahms was seriously ill, went to Vienna to visit him in the middle of March 1897. It was the last meeting of these two great friends. Brahms died shortly afterwards, on the 2nd April 1897, and Dvořák, in the company of other notable personalities, attended his funeral.— Suk's Quartet in B flat major, op. 11.—Our Quartet: the Bohemian Quartet.

205. DVOŘÁK'S COMPOSITIONS IN AMSTERDAM

... This evening I got a letter from Suk. Last Sunday there was a great sensation at the Philharmonic Concert in Amsterdam. The whole concert was dedicated exclusively to my compositions. 1. "In Nature's Realm" (overture), 2. the Violin Concerto (Hoffmann), the "From the New World" Symphony. Suk, Nedbal and Wihan have only the best to say of the performance under Mengelberg's baton...

Dvořák to Simrock in Berlin, 21. II. 1898.—The concert in Amsterdam, conducted by the Dutch conductor, *Wilhelm Mengelberg* (1871-1951) took place on Februar 13th 1898. The Violin Concerto was played by the leader of the Bohemian Quartet, *Karel Hoffmann* (see 183).

206. GOOD NEWS AGAIN FROM RICHTER

Honoured Friend,

Queen's Hotel, Eastbourne.
June 7th, 1898.

Your "New World" Symphony gave us all great delight again at my 2nd Concert in London on the fourth of this month.— In Paris, too, your "Carnival" took on very well and had a great success with the public. What have you got this year for our Philharmonic in Vienna? I shall be at home from the 20th of this month, if you have any news for me.

With best greetings, Your devoted

Hans Richter.

Hans Richter in Eastbourne to Dvořák at Vysoká.—For the performance of the "Carnival" Overture with the Colonne Orchestra in Paris see 198.

207. TWO MORE SYMPHONIC POEMS

Prague, June 22nd 1898.

Honoured Friend,

A thousand thanks for your kind letter from Paris and from London and the same measure of thanks for your performance of my "Carnival" Overture and the "New World" Symphony in both these cities.

You ask me if I have anything new? Certainly, not much but at least something. Two new Symphonic Poems, both still in manuscript but the score and parts are at your disposal straight away. Even if the two works should be engraved by autumn, I shall arrange with Simrock for you to be able to play the composition in Vienna from manuscript. One takes about 25 minutes —"The Wild Dove", the other will probably be entitled "The Hero's Song". Neither have yet been played anywhere.

If I knew that you would be staying in Vienna in summer, I should like very much to bring you the things so that we could go through them.

I have been in Prague for a fortnight and am leaving on Friday for Vysoká by Příbram where I shall remain till autumn. All correspondence will be sent on to me at Vysoká and if you should want anything, all letters will reach me there.

Are you in Bayreuth? This summer I should really like to go there.

So once more my best thanks for all the tokens of your goodwill and send word soon to your sincere friend and admirer,

Antonín Dvořák.

Dvořák to Hans Richter in Vienna.—For a correct report of Richter's concerts in Paris see 200.—The two new Symphonic Poems: *"The Wild Dove"*, op. 110, was written between the 22nd October and the 18th November 1896, *"The Hero's Song"*, op. 111, between the 4th August and the 25th October 1897.—To visit the Wagner Festival in Bayreuth was Dvořák's long-cherished but apparently never realized wish (see also 235).

208. A NEW INTERPRETER – GUSTAV MAHLER

Highly honoured Master, Vienna, Oct. 3rd 1898.

As you may perhaps know, I have taken over the direction of the Philharmonic Concerts, and, as I have been told that you have just finished a new work, I take the liberty of asking you to entrust the Philharmonic with its first performance. I should be greatly indebted to you for a favourable answer.

Your devoted

Mahler.

Gustav Mahler in Vienna to Dvořák in Prague.—In 1898, Richter resigned from his post as conductor of the Vienna Philharmonic and was succeeded by Gustav Mahler (1860-1911), from 1897 also the new director of the Hofoper in Vienna.

209. FAMILY CELEBRATIONS

18 3/11 98.

Dearest Friend,

This is to let you know that on the 17th November of this year, we shall celebrate our Silver Wedding and at the same time the marriage of our Otilka to Mr. Suk, a member of the Czech Quartet.

It would give us great pleasure to have you with us on that day, and so I beg you, if it is at all possible, come—do come!

With warmest greetings, Yours,

Antonín Dvořák.

Dvořák in Prague to A. Rus (see 81) *in Písek.*—The wedding of the composer Josef Suk (see 1) and Dvořák's eldest daughter, Otilie, took place on the 17th November 1898.

Dearest Friend,

... That I have work and cares more than enough I do not need to tell you, indeed I am now so distracted that my work is not making any great progress. I have two acts complete in score and am now working at the third, but as I said, it is going ahead slowly and I don't see much progress.

I wonder if you know that my new Symphonic Poems, "The Wild Dove" and "The Hero's Song" are to be performed in Vienna.

The Director of the Opera, Gustav Mahler, is conducting the Philharmonic, as Richter's successor, and he wrote to me a short time ago asking whether I had something new?—I replied that I had two new compositions and he wrote at once in reply: "Also schicken Sie mir beide Werke."

And so I did and both will be played for the first time in Vienna, but in Prague, too, I expect, in due course.

Today's papers contain the announcement of our wedding and congratulations are pouring in from all sides.

Wedding cards have been sent to England, Germany, Holland etc. If you saw the mountains of envelopes—some hundreds at the least—you would be horrified. They worked at it for several days.

Oh well, small pains small gains!—

Your affectionate and sincere Friend,

Antonín Dvořák.

Dvořák to A. Göbl (see 33) *at Sychrov.*—My work: the composition of the opera "The Devil and Kate" (see 201).—For Mahler's performance of Dvořák's works in Vienna see 208.

23. Leoš Janáček.

24. Dvořák (1886).

211. MAHLER KEEPS HIS WORD

Highly honoured Master,   Vienna, 17th Nov. 1898.

I have just received your second work "The Hero's Song" and, as with the first, am quite enchanted with it. If you agree, I shall perform "The Hero's Song" first at the 3rd Philharmonic Concert on the 4th December. Rehearsals will begin in the week preceding the 4th December and I should be very pleased if you could be present not only at the performance but also at the rehearsals. Be so kind, then, as to let me know when you are coming.

Your devoted

Mahler.

Gustav Mahler (see 208) *in Vienna to Dvořák in Prague.*—Dvořák sent to Vienna "The Wild Dove" and "The Hero's Song" and Mahler accepted and performed both works: first "The Hero's Song", on December 4th 1898, the composer being present at this the first performance of the work, and then "The Wild Dove" on December 3rd 1899.

212. SUCCESS OF "THE DEVIL AND KATE"

My dear, good Friend,

I have long been wanting to write to you again but you know how very busy I have been lately, what with the composition of my new opera, and then rehearsals and constant nervous strain so that I really was not properly disposed to sit down and write. So the opera was given on the evening of Thursday, the 23rd, and on Sunday evening again, and was attended by a big audience and with such success as I had not expected to see in our days. To write about it is, I think, unnecessary, for you are sure to have read in the newspapers about how the première turned out.

The opera thus found decided favour. First of all it was well received by the soloists, orchestra and choir, then by the public and all the critics, with a few exceptions. The opera went off splendidly, soloists, orchestra and choir all did their part with enthusiasm, which made me very happy, and if I had a text today I should set to work again with a will.

On Sunday the Philharmonic is playing my "Wild Dove", which seems to have had a sensational success in London a short time ago. At least according to reports I read in our newspapers taken from the London papers. I am just writing there now to thank them for the invitation to come—but, unfortunately, I probably shall not be able to go this time as they are giving "The Devil and Kate" on Sunday, Dec. 3rd, for the fourth time and I must stay here for it as I have word that Hanslick has written to Prague that somebody, if not he himself, will be here.

I must tell you, too, that I was in Berlin. The Philharmonic there performed my "Hero's Song" on the 13th November and Nikisch of Leipzig conducted it. I was to conduct it personally the following day, but I was so indisposed that I had to leave Berlin with my wife—without even seeing Simrock.

Nikisch was greatly taken with "The Hero's Song", proof of which is that he also played it in Hamburg and is playing it in Leipzig on the 30th November and even wishes me to be there. Perhaps you know, too, that I shall also be conducting in Budapest. I shall conduct "The Hero's Song", Wihan is to play the Cello Concerto and then there will be the "Carnival" Overture. In addition, there is to be a so-called "Dvořák Evening" at which our Quartet will play, and Friend Heš from Vienna will sing.

So you see how fond people are of me everywhere, isn't that so? We got the biscuits and I am to send you many thanks from my wife and children.

Yours affectionately,

Antonín Dvořák.

18 27/12 99.

From Dvořák in Prague to A. Göbl (see 33) *at Sychrov.*—The première of the opera "The Devil and Kate" took place at the National Theatre in Prague on November 23rd 1899.—*Arthur Nikisch* (see 160) was conductor of the Gewandhaus Concerts in Leipzig from 1895, and, at the same time, conducted the concerts of the Berlin Philharmonic. Dvořák cancelled his engagement to conduct "The Hero's Song" because of a sudden nervous breakdown.—The concert of the Philharmonic Society in Budapest took place on December 20th 1899, with Dvořák present. The concert devoted to Dvořák's works, was given by the Bohemian Quartet, with the co-operation of the Viennese Hofoper singer, Vilém Heš, and the famous violinist, Jan Kubelík, on the evening before.

213. DVOŘÁK ON HIS COMPOSITIONS

Dear Friend,

I looked for and have found the analysis of "The Wild Dove" by Janáček of Brno—but the main motif of the youth "Trumpet in the distance" is not there-and must be there.

It can also be played in the orchestra—but the distance must be properly tested from where the youth's call comes... In any case, the trumpets must play *forte* so that the audience can hear it. Then I am sending you Kretschmar's analysis of the Symphony, but the nonsense—that I made use of "Indian" and American motifs—leave out, because it is a lie, I only sought to write in the spirit of these American folk-melodies.

But in any case do as you think best. You still have the *tempi* well in mind and that is the chief thing. Take the Introduction to the Symphony as "leisurely" as possible.

Thank you for your kindness,

I remain, Always your sincere friend,

A. Dvořák.

Greetings to the Suks. Why don't they write?
Give my greeetings to Hofman and Wihánek, too.

Dvořák in Prague to Oskar Nedbal in Amsterdam, February 1900.—On the initi-
ative of Fritz Simrock, a symphony concert of Dvořák's compositions was held in Berlin
on March 2nd 1900, at which the Berlin Philharmonic played the "From the New
World" Symphony, the Violin Concerto with Karel Hoffmann, the Symphonic Poem,
"The Wild Dove" and the "Carnival" Overture, with Oskar Nedbal (see 158) conduct-
ing. In addition the programme included songs sung by the Russian singer, Ida Ekman.
—Nedbal, who at the time was on a concert tour as viola-player with the Bohemian
Quartet in Holland, asks Dvořák to send him an analysis of "The Wild Dove" by Ja-
náček of Brno (see 14) and of the Symphony by Hermann Kretzschmar from the series
"Führer durch den Konzertsaal".—Dvořák was not present at the Berlin concert.

214. DVOŘÁK'S OPERATIC MASTERPIECE "RUSALKA"

In autumn of the year 1899, when I wrote the libretto
"Rusalka", I had no idea that I was writing it for Antonín
Dvořák. I wrote it not knowing for whom...It is true that my
secret wish was that it might come to Dvořák's notice but I did
not dare to approach him...Till one day at Christmas-time, the
office of the National Theatre published a notice in the papers
that Dvořák was looking for a new libretto through the agency
of the National Theatre. I went to Director Šubert and told him
that I had a libretto. I think it was the next day we had an
appointment with Dvořák at the Director's office beside the
stage, and Dvořák, who always had absolute confidence in
Šubert's judgment, listened attentively to his opinion of my
Rusalka and took my manuscript home with him. The recommendation of Director Šubert thus decided the matter...

Rusalka was composed during the year 1900. Dvořák accepted my text as it was written and I only had to insert something new into the first act: Rusalka's Song "Wisdom of Ages"
at the feet of the old Witch. I have the happiest recollections of
my contact with Dvořák at that time from whom I also have two
interesting letters. I think that what brought me close to Dvořák
was our love for Erben, and that the atmosphere of Erben's
Ballads which I tried to communicate to Rusalka, meant more

for Dvořák than the actual libretto. At this time Dvořák often came to see me; he would come not seldom after seven o'clock in the morning, in fact sometimes he had to get somebody to call me, and then he was already on his way back from his morning round of the Prague railway-stations where he went to look at the locomotives. Usually he would begin to speak about anything and everything but his opera: either about the engines he had just been inspecting or about pigeons— in short, about everything possible that had nothing to do with the libretto. Then he would forget why he had come, light the stump of his cigar—and without warning went as he had come without having come to the point.

In the meantime I had become literary adviser to the National Theatre; and then he went to see me there. Sometimes he came with a terrible worry and, at times, with questions that left me at a loss for an answer. I remember one such conversation. In the Third Act of "Rusalka", the mad Prince has the following lines:

"—on Heaven and Earth I lay my curse,
I curse both god and spirits all,
Answer then, answer now my call!"

This did not please Dvořák at all. He said to me: "Listen, I am a believer. I can't curse God in my music." And I had to go into a long explanation that the libretto does not in any way force him to do that and that "to curse god" is not to curse the Lord God. He allowed himself to be persuaded and composed to the words as I had written them.

First thing in the morning after the première, Dvořák called in to see us at the Theatre office in the best of moods. Straight away on seeing me, he calls out: "And now, quick, quick a new libretto!" I reply: "I haven't any, Master." And he: "Then write something quick as long as I feel like it and a nice role for Maturová."

I promised. Yes, I promised. But I did not keep my word.

*From the article by Jaroslav Kvapil "The Birth of Rusalka".—*After the successful première of the opera "The Devil and Kate", Dvořák longed to compose another operatic work and it was no small stroke of good fortune that there came into his hands a libretto so poetically sensitive and musically inspirational as the libretto of the fairy-tale opera "Rusalka" by the young Czech poet and playwright, *Jaroslav Kvapil* (1868-1950), later the chief stage-manager and director of the National Theatre in Prague, with a deservedly high reputation. The plot of this fairy-tale is adapted from Andersen's tale of the water-nymph who greatly desires the love of a man-prince, but hawing been disappointed in her love, brings about her own destruction and that of her lover.— Dvořák who, in a wonderful way, has embodied in his music the magic poetry of the fairy-tale and the peculiar charm and fascination of its emotional tension, has created in "Rusalka" his greatest dramatic work. He was engaged in its composition from April 21st to November 27th 1900. The première at the National Theatre in Prague took place on March 31st 1901 under the direction of the chef d'opera, *Karel Kovařovic* (see 127). The celebrated *Karel Burian* (1870-1924) and *Bohumil Pták* (1869-1933), then tenors at the National Theatre in Prague, *Růžena Maturová* (1869-1938), primadonna and the first Rusalka, which was one of her best rôles.

215. MAHLER'S INTEREST IN "RUSALKA"

K. und K. Hofoper Theater.

Z 313

1901

Vienna, the 4th May, 1901.

Honoured Sir,

After looking through the piano arrangement which the Czech Theatre was kind enough to send me, I should very much like to count on performing your opera Rusalka but would need first of all the German text. I therefore take the liberty of asking you to be good enough to let me know if you have such a translation or if you intend to have a translation made and to whom I should address myself in the matter.

Thanking you for your kind reply to my letter,

I am, with the expression of my deep respect,

Your most devoted

Mahler,

K. und K. Direktor des Hofoper Theaters.

Gustav Mahler (see 208) *in Vienna to Dvořák in Prague.—*His letter is the beginning of long negotiations about the performance of "Rusalka" at the Hofoper in Vienna which, in spite of all Mahler's efforts, did not come to anything. The libretto of "Rusalka" was translated into German by the Viennese writer, Josa Will.

216. DVOŘÁK IN THE AUSTRIAN SENATE

. . . Dvořák made his entry into the Senate (Herrenhaus), along with Emil Frída, on March 14th 1901. That was the real name of Jaroslav Vrchlický and that name alone was used in all the documents and speeches of the Austrian Senate in which he was mentioned. It was truly a strange coincidence that the raising of the greatest contemporary poet and the greatest contemporary composer of the Czech nation to the peerage should become part of a political action whereby Dr. Körber wanted in some measure to placate the dissatisfaction of the Czech people dating from October 18th 1899, when the Language Decrees of Badeni and Gautsch were annulled and when Czech was completely abolished from the internal administration of local and central Government offices and law courts in Bohemia and Moravia.

Dvořák and Vrchlický entered the Viennese Senate together. They were first presented in accordance with custom, to the President, Prince Alfred Windischgrätz, then led to their seats by Mr. Wohanka. All eyes were turned on them. They were in morning dress, each had round his neck the large medal of honour, Litteris and Artibus. The two full-bearded Dioscuri, were a truly rare sight among the company that filled the Austrian Senate. They had nothing, alone the glory of their names famed throughout the whole world. They were indebted for nothing to any of their forefathers—only to themselves, their genius and their work. On all sides there was keen curiosity as to how this musician and this poet, this writer of symphonies and this writer of lyrics, would acquit themselves in the field of legislative activity. At that time they took the oath in Czech, for then it was a matter of course. Each member of the Austrian Senate had in front of him a writing-desk, an inkpot, a sand-sprinkler, blotting-paper, several pens and several pencils, Hardtmut no 2, soft and yet not brittle, the best product of its kind. Dvořák was greatly delighted with these pencils. He took them all and put them in his pocket. Having left the Senate

House, he showed his booty to his wife who was waiting for him and said: "Look that will be grand composing now!" And when she asked him what he and Vrchlický had done on their début in the Parliamentary lists, he replied triumphantly: "We cut them all to ribbons!" That day Dvořák voted in the Senate for the first and last time. He never appeared there again. His seat remained deserted...

From "Antonín Dvořák as Politician", by Josef Penížek (1858-1932), the Viennese correspondent of the Prague daily, "Národní listy". — Dvořák and, along with him, the great Czech poet, Jaroslav Vrchlický were appointed, on April 14th 1901, members of the Austrian Senate (Herrenhaus). The session at which they were presented was held on May 14th of the same year. Count Badeni, Dr. Von Körber, Paul Gautsch: Prime Ministers of the Austrian Government; Josef Wohanka, Czech politician and member of the Senate.—Litteris et artibus; a distinction awarded to Dvořák by the Austrian Emperor in November 1898.

217. PUBLIC HONOURS

... Dvořák received the congratulations of the public (on his appointment as a member of the Austrian Senate) by a happy coincidence of circumstances in a way which will scarcely present itself again to the Prague musical community of both nations - on the occasion of a concert given on April 15th by the Berlin Philharmonic. It was the occasion of a manifestation such as no other artist on the international concert tour of this excellent body of musicians will be vouchsafed. After the Symphonic Poem "The Wild Dove", the conductor, Arthur Nikisch, shook the thunderous applause from his own person and with a gesture of his hands, transferred it to the composer present in the box of the President of the Czech Academy, Josef Hlávka. The whole Philharmonic Orchestra rose to their feet and applauded when Dvořák came forward to the balustrade to thank the audience and the artists for the honour shown him but there was still no end to the unanimous jubilation till the Master appeared on the platform where he was welcomed with stormy ovations and was recalled again and again.

218. ANNIVERSARY CELEBRATIONS IN VIENNA

Dear and Beloved Master,

You see you should have been here yesterday. The Viennese missed you very, very much. It was a success that it plucked at one's very heart-strings. I am so very fond of you that I thought to myself that I was maybe not objective enough. That goes for Nedbal, too, when I heard how splendidly your t ings sounded under his baton, but when I looked round me in t he hall I had no need to fear that it was only I who liked them. The people were jubilant and the best Viennese audience was there—German. That the Czechs were beside themselves with joy goes without saying.

Three Ministers, among them the Minister of Education, were present and all were carried away. They said to me personally how lovely and splendid it was.

The enclosed cuttings are proof that I am not the only one who holds you in such high respect and is so fond of you. I am sending them at the request of Nedbal and Mr. Hoffmann so that you will have to believe them when they tell you how successful everything was.

The orchestra played with enthusiasm.

I am, Respectfully and devotedly, Your

Greif.

Vienna, 18/12 1901.

Emanuel Greif, Czech Civil Servant in the Austrian Presidium of Ministers in Vienna, *to Dvořák in Prague.*—On the occasion of Dvořák's 60th birthday, there was held in Vienna, on the 17th December 1901, a Jubilee Concert by the Czech Philharmonic under Oskar Nedbal (see 158), with a programme including the "Carnival" Overture, the Violin Concerto, with Karel Hoffmann as soloist, and the Symphony, "From the New World".

219. RICHTER–AN ENTHUSIASTIC PROPAGATOR

Dearly esteemed Friend,

After the great delight which your D major Symphony gave us all yesterday, I feel I must write you a few lines. I do not know whether you are informed that in Manchester and the towns through which I am travelling with my orchestra we are very much engaged with your compositions; your name is among those that appear in my programmes most frequently. I am writing this to you because I think it gives you pleasure, not, however, to win your praise. It is my *duty* to devote all my talent to the propagating and support of good and beautiful works; and you make the fulfilment of that duty easy and delightful. So no word of thanks or I shall not send you any more programmes...

I am proud that you should have honoured me with the dedication of this magnificent symphony. I shall perform it at my London concerts–in May of this year–again; it will be its *second* London performance; the first was years ago, immediately after its publication.

Shall I not perhaps see you at Bayreuth? *You mustn't fail to be there!*

With best greetings to your whole family,
Your devoted
Hans Richter.

Richter in England to Dvořák in Prague, 24. I. 1902.—For the dedication to Richter of the D major Symphony see 37, 45, 53 and 54.—For the visit to Bayreuth see 207.

220. A RARE PERIOD OF CREATIVE INACTIVITY

Dear Friend,   19 11/2 02.

I cannot say how glad I should be to do what you ask me, and how glad I should be to come and see you again at Kromě-říž—but I expect it will be in vain to decide to do it— I have been *without work* for more than 14 months, I cannot *make up my mind* to anything and I do not know how long my present state will last—as long as I do not find what I am seeking for I must put everything else aside, and so I cannot promise you anything, for which I am very sorry. Perhaps you could ask Mr. Nedbal, I am sure he would be very pleased to do it. Please do not be angry with me and apologize for me to the gentlemen of the "Moravan" and ask them to excuse me.

I also had an invitation from Leipzig from the Gewand-haus and then from Prof. Klengl—he played my" Cello Concerto," but I declined that there, too,—

With kind regards to your wife and warm greetings to yourself,

I remain, Your

Ant. Dvořák.

Dvořák to Dr. Emil Kozánek (see 159) *in Kroměříž.*—14 months without work: i. e. from the completion of "Rusalka" at the end of November 1900.—*Julius Klengel* (1859-1933), famous German violoncellist, soloist at the Gewandhaus Concerts in Leipzig.

221. DVOŘÁK AND MEYERBEER

... "Master Dvořák was fond of Meyerbeer, that's music for you, he would say. We were studying "Les Huguenots" and after a piano rehearsal when I was leaving the theatre, Dvořák stopped me: "I heard some strains of Meyerbeer, I am looking forward to it." During the first performance, Kovařovic came to me in the interval and said that Dvořák was looking for me, that he was enthusiastic about it and must tell me so. At that moment I hear Dvořák's voice in the passage: "Mařák, Mařák, where is Mařák?" I ran out and called: "I am here, Master." Dvořák quite red in the face with excitement looked at me but said nothing, and so I asked him: "Is there anything you wish, Master?" Dvořák looked at me a little while longer and then said brusquely: "No, nothing," and went off.

From "*Reminiscences of Antonín Dvořák.*" by the celebrated Czech tenor, *Otakar Mařák* (1872-1939), who, at the new production of the opera "Les Huguenots" on the 26th March 1903, sang the role of Raul.

222. DVOŘÁK AND CHARPENTIER

When Charpentier's "Louisa" was celebrating its first triumphs, Dvořák often used to come to the café with a piano arrangement of this opera under his arm. Once, having come later than he, I found him sitting engrossed in the study of this opera. On seeing me, he nodded for me to sit down beside him, whereupon with serious mien he drew my attention to a certain place: "Look at that there, Charpentier is a strange kind of musician. Everywhere false notes. For instance, where there should be C he has C sharp, where A flat he has A. Then this chord here, you can see at once that it's wrong." Suddenly, as if he had just remembered that I was his former pupil, he said: "Now, how would you do it better?" I diffidently gave my opinion. But Dvořák looked at me with disdain, and, pointing to the chord in question, said: "*No—it's right like that!*"

A reminiscence recorded by *Josef Faměra* (1883-1914), a Czech pianist who often accompanied František Ondříček on his concert tours.—Charpentier's opera "Louisa" was performed by the Prague National Theatre for the first time on February 13th 1903.—It is apparent that Dvořák was very interested in the work also from the fact that after the première he bought the piano arrangement of the work and studied it attentively as is to be seen from the marginal comments, approving and disapproving, entered in his handwriting.

223. AT WORK ON A NEW OPERA

... I am now working at a big opera with words by Dr. Jaroslav Vrchlický (Armida) and am happy that after such a long rest I can work again at something that I want and not that others want.

Today I received a contract from Director Mahler regarding the performance of Rusalka at the Hofoper and I firmly hope that it will take place in autumn.

Looking forward to seeing you in Vienna, I am, with great respect,

Your deeply obliged and devoted

Antonín Dvořák.

Dvořák to the Czech Minister in Vienna, Dr. Antonín Rezek, in autumn 1902.— The opera "Armida" for which Jaroslav Vrchlický wrote the libretto—an episode from the romance of the Princess of Damascus, Armida, the Crusading knight, Rinald, and the Syrian sorcerer, Ismen, after Tasso's "Jerusalem Liberated", was Dvořák's last work and was composed between March 11th 1902 and June 29th 1903.

224. DVOŘÁK'S LAST CREATIVE PLAN

Dear Sir,

I have had your libretto "Horymír" in my hands for a long time and I thank you for sending me the book. I have read it and it interests me. I shall have to read it more often before I can decide and then I should discuss the matter with you. I do not promise anything but I should be glad if I could again start to work on a new dramatic composition. As you perhaps know I have just now finished a big opera by Jaroslav Vrchlický (Armida) and I have again come to the conclusion that it is good and neccessary for the composer to discuss everything orally with the librettist, where it is necessary to shorten

or again to add something or change it altogether. As you, however, are far from Prague, that will not be possible and so I
think that when I am back in Prague after the holidays, I shall
come, if there is a station there, and see you. But it would be
good if you would put into the libretto what is absolutely essen-
tial for me.

That is, mainly the stage directions—what is happening and
how—for the principal characters, to indicate clearly when they
come on and when they leave the stage. There is a great deal of
that and it is entirely missing in the libretto. So I shall read
in your libretto again and again, maybe a number of times every
day, till I get a complete grasp of it, and I assure you once more
that it would give me great pleasure to be able to decide again
for a dramatic work, and if it should be "Horymír", it would
give me special pleasure.

Antonín Dvořák.

Dvořák in Vysoká to Ing. Dr. Rud. Stárek (1872-1920) in Lang-Enzensdorf by
Vienna, 20. VII. 1903.—Dr. Stárek wrote several librettos for operas and the libretto
"Horymír", based on a Czech legend, which he offered to Dvořák. As the above letter
shows, Dvořák was seriously interested in the libretto and soon after finishing "Armida"
began to make sketches of some of the basic thematic motifs. They were the last mani-
festations of his creative spirit.

225. THE VYSOKÁ MINERS AND "HORYMÍR".

... I have happy memories of the end of the holidays in 1903
when my Father had the libretto prepared for the new opera
"Horymír" and had even made a number of sketches for it.
At Vysoká he told the miners that he was going to write an
opera and that in one act there would be real miners and that
they would work in the mine with exactly the same machines
as they worked with in the Příbram and Březohorské mines.
And then Father promised them that at the première of the

opera the National Theatre must give him the whole auditorium where the miners from Příbram would take their places as the main part of the audience so that they might give their opinion about how far the act gives the impression of reality. The miners expressed their doubts as they thought that it would be very difficult to show a whole mine at the theatre with all its beauties and terrors. Then Father would tell them that all that was the business of the stage director to see that it was right and assured the miners that it must be possible when there are operas where whole acts are played under water or when, as in one of his operas, a real Hell is conjured up on the stage, and real devils with tails.

A reminiscence recorded by the Master's son Otakar, in "Ant. Dvořák in his Relations with Vysoká and its Miners."—See 223.—The plot of the opera "Horymír" was to have been set partly in the mines of Březové Hory near Dvořák's summer residence at Vysoká. This may partly explain Dvořák's interest in the libretto.

226. DVOŘÁK'S ABSORPTION IN DRAMATIC MUSIC

... In the last five years I have written nothing but operas. I wanted to devote all my powers, as long as God gives me the health, to the creation of opera. Not, however, out of any vain desire for glory but because I consider opera the most suitable form for the nation. This music is listened to by the broad masses, whereas when I compose a symphony I might have to wait years for it to be performed. I got a request again from Simrock for chamber works which I keep refusing. My publishers know by now that I shall no longer write anything just for them. They bombard me with questions why I do not compose this or that; these genres have no longer any attraction for me. They look upon me as a composer of symphonies and yet I proved to them long years ago that my main bias is towards dramatic creation.—

From an interview with Dvořák for the Vienna daily, "Die Reichswehr", 1.III.1904.

227. DVOŘÁK THE MUSICAL DRAMATIST

... I was among those who in Dvořák's compositions always felt and recognized all the signs of great expressive powers for dramatic music.

From the essay: "Czech Musical Trends" by Leoš Janáček (see 14).

228. THE LAST CONTACT WITH LONDON

"After Armida can we expect another opera from you?"
—Yes. I have three texts here, two Czech things and one with a Turko-Bulgarian theme; I do not know yet for which material I shall decide.

Other offers I reject without exception. I got a splendid offer this season from Berlin. I was to go on a big concert tour with the Berlin Philharmonic through Austria, Germany, France and Italy. In London they offered me the direction of the Popular Concerts of which one concert was to be of my own compositions and I was also to appear as a pianist. Especially as regards the latter, I hesitated very much, because I do not feel so sure of myself as a pianist as to dare to undertake a public appearance. I have also been asked to conduct concerts in Lvov and Warsaw but I declined all these offers as I did not wish to bind myself...

From an interview for the "Reichswehr" (see 226).

229. DVOŘÁK AS PIANIST (I.)

Dvořák was not by any means a piano virtuoso, he had not acquired the technique for that, but his playing was sound, full of feeling and manly. He did not "thump" (as is usual with untrained players) and when he played things which he had to practise, as for instance the Dumky, he showed remarkable feeling for fine differences of touch and in pedal technique. With him I often played new works of his and various other composers, as duets, mostly from score–I at the top and he at the bottom, and it went very well because he read scores, even complicated ones, with remarkable ease. Sometimes I was in his way, and then he finished it himself. And even though, in the most complicated passages, he "swindled" a little as we say, it always gave a definite idea of the whole and the same was the case when he played over his pupils' things from score. Moreover he had a very exact notion of how a thing should be played; he was severe in his demands on pianists and also had his ideas about how to compose for piano. He liked the piano and used to say: "Good music must also sound well on the piano." In his last period (I mean after Rusalka) he did not compose at the piano nor in his young days when he had no piano. And with what fire he then played it over!–When we used to play his pince-nez would often fall at the forte passages and he used to abuse it roundly. He seldom played the piano arrangement of his things for four hands, but when we sometimes played them he stood behind us and tapped various things in time with us on our backs and made practical demands as regards tempo and touch, at times it was too loud for him, then again it was not with sufficient feeling, or again he wanted an orchestral ff, but no "thumping"...

From a letter by Josef Suk (see 1).

230. DVOŘÁK AS PIANIST (II.)

I recall that before I came to know the Master personally I often heard it said that he was no pianist. It was perhaps true but only from the strictly virtuoso point of view. Dvořák was not a virtuoso but he had a very fair command of the piano along with a musicality which was peculiarly his. At least as regards playing from score I can boldly affirm that the accuracy with which he played a score from sight might be the envy of many a piano virtuoso. I do not know, however, how he acquired this confidence in playing from score but I think he achieved it not so much from the study of scores by other composers, as in his own compositional work and his remarkable genius for combination. Later he himself made an interesting comment in this connection. "When I play from score," he said, "I follow the top part and the bass, and from that I can imagine what is in between."

Josef Michl (see 4): "*My First Lesson with Antonín Dvořák.*"

231. AN INVITATION

19 26/2 04.

Dear Friend,

I am looking forward very much to your arrival in Prague. The main rehearsals are on Monday at 10 a. m. and on Tuesday *the dress rehearsal* (10 a. m.).

With kind regards, Your

Antonín Dvořák.

Dvořák to Leoš Janáček (see 14) *in Brno.*

232. DVOŘÁK FEARS ILLNESS

He was afraid of his illness. At the beginning of 1904 we were sitting in the Imperial (café) when Dvořák entered. His face was overcast and he complained of a pain in his side. The doctor says that it is lumbago. The composer, Malát, who was present said well–meaningly: "Sometimes they say it's lumbago. My brother-in-law had a pain like that and they said, too, that it was lumbago but it was the kidneys, and my brother-in-law died within a month." Dvořák got terribly angry. "What are you telling me that for? Was anybody asking you about it? You want to frighten me." etc, he thundered out at the unhappy Malát who, unfortunately, proved to be right...

From "Musical Memoirs" by Ladislav Dolanský (see 73).—Jan Malát, Czech musical pedagogue and composer (1843-1915).

233. DVOŘÁK SERIOUSLY ILL

Dvořák, on hearing the name Dr. Kozánek, gladly admitted us to his presence (3. IV. 1904, in the forenoon). We went in. The Master was lying on a sofa and received us with great friendliness. He himself began to tell us that he was somewhat ailing but that it wasn't so bad. He was looking forward to getting quite better in Dr. Kozánek's comfortable household. Then Dvořák got up and sat down at the table where we were sitting and began to tell us about things of everyday interest; as regards musical matters, he touched upon his latest composition and his plans for the future. During this conversation, he showed great mental alertness and mentioned several times how he was looking forward to Kroměříž. Then we took our leave of him. We left the Master's house in a depressed mood. We gave the house in which the Master lived one more glance and looked at each other with foreboding in our eyes. The eyes of both of us were bright with tears. And why? After all Dvořák was not dangerously ill.—After some time Dr. Kozánek said: "If only we don't lose him!" — It was an affecting moment...

From the recollections of Ferdinand Vach (1860-1939), founder and for many years conductor of the famous "Choral Union of Moravian Teachers".—*Dr. Emil Kozánek* see 159.—The Choral and Musical Society "Moravan" in Kroměříž in Moravia were preparing for a performance of Dvořák's ballad, "The Spectre's Bride", to take place on the 7th and 8th May 1904, with the composer conducting, and Vach, along with Kozánek, went to visit Dvořák, when in Prague to attend the first Czech Musical Festival, which was held on the 3rd and 4th of March 1904. At this Festival, performances were given of Dvořák's oratorio "Saint Ludmilla", the Symphony "From the New World" and the Violin Concerto in which František Ondříček was the soloist. Dvořák himself was prevented by illness from taking part in the Festival.

234. DVOŘÁK'S DEATH

A month ago Master Dvořák lay down not to rise again. The celebrations of the Festival which were opened as a mark of honour with his noble oratorio "Saint Ludmilla" and at which the outstanding works of his other creative production were fittingly represented—these celebrations he was unable to attend. His strong, healthy body was struck down by a heart stroke when bladder trouble and influenza had already confined him to his bed. As the Master felt easier yesterday, the doctor, after 10 days in which he had not left his bed, allowed him to get up to his dinner. His wife and son Otakar dressed him and with their help he sat down in his chair and ate a plate of soup with unusual zest. Scarcely had he finished when he said: "I feel kind of giddy. I think I had better go and lie down." These were the Master's last words, for on the instant he turned pale and then dark red and fell back in his chair. He wanted to say something but only unintelligible sounds came from his throat. His pulse was still to be felt and then was very weak and finally stopped altogether, and the doctor, who had been sent for in haste, could only certify the Master's death.

Report in the Czech musical magazine "Dalibor".—Dvořák died in his Prague home at midday on May 1st 1904.

235. A SERIOUS LOSS FOR THE MUSICAL WORLD

... The Warsaw Philharmonic changed the programme of its Symphony Concert. In honour of his memory they included the "Hussite" of the great Czech composer, Dr. Antonín Dvořák, of whose death news has just come in. I stand uncertainly with the others in the crowded foyer. Is it then true that he should have died?

From reminiscences by Leoš Janáček (see 14).—The news of Dvořák's death spread rapidly throughout the whole world and awakened, especially in musical circles, exceptional feeling, for it was realized that not only the greatest living Czech composer had passed away but one of the greatest and most famous composers in the world.

It was unfortunately true. Dvořák was dead...

But his work has not died. This work, nourished by honest Czech musicianship and strengthened by the gift of creative genius, has swelled to a mighty song of ecstatic love for life and its Creator, —a song which, for its pure and enduring beauty and for its individual flavour imbued so unmistakably with the spirit of the artist's country, is received with love and gratitude wherever it is heard and in every part of the globe.

The path along which this work gradually grew, the remarkable path of Dvořák's life, did not in its singular rise to glory blaze into sight like a comet only shortly to be extinguished, but marks a permanent victory, the fruits of which are one of the happiest achievements that Czech art and Czech culture have given to the world.

O. Š.

LIST OF ILLUSTRATIONS

17. Dvořák in the robes of an honorary doctor of Cambridge University.
18. Jeanette Thurber.
19. *S. S. Saale* on which Dvořák sailed to America and returned again to Europe three years later.
20. Facsimile of a page from the sketch for the Symphony "From the New World".
21. School and church in Spillville, America.
22. The Kneisel Quartet in Boston.
23. Leoš Janáček.
24. Dvořák (1886).
Opposite the title page: Antonín Dvořák (1878).

ANTONÍN DVOŘÁK

LETTERS AND REMINISCENCES

Translated from the Czech
by Roberta Finlayson-Samsour
Published by Artia, Prague, Czechoslovakia